WINNING STRATEGIES
for Classroom
Management

CAROL CUMMINGS

Association for Supervision
and Curriculum Development

Alexandria, Virginia USA

Association for Supervision and Curriculum Development
1703 N. Beauregard St. • Alexandria, VA 22311-1714 USA
Telephone: 1-800-933-2723 or 703-578-9600 • Fax: 703-575-5400
Web site: http://www.ascd.org • E-mail: member@ascd.org

Michelle Terry, *Deputy Executive Director, Program Development*
Nancy Modrak, *Director of Publishing*
John O'Neil, *Director of Acquisitions*
Joyce McLeod, *Development Editor*
Julie Houtz, *Managing Editor of Books*
Darcie Russell, *Associate Editor*
Ernesto Yermoli, *Project Assistant*
Gary Bloom, *Director, Design and Production Services*
Karen Monaco, *Senior Designer*
Tracey A. Smith, *Production Manager*
Dina Murray Seamon, *Production Coordinator*
Vivian L. Coss, *Production Coordinator*

Printed in the United States of America.

August 2000 member book (p). ASCD Premium, Comprehensive, and Regular members
periodically receive ASCD books as part of their membership benefits. No. FY99-09.

ASCD Product No. 100052
ASCD member price: $17.95   nonmember price: $21.95

Library of Congress Cataloging-in-Publication Data
Cummings, Carol Bradford.
   Winning strategies for classroom management / by Carol Cummings.
      p. cm.
Includes bibliographical references and index.
   ISBN 0-87120-381-2
   1. Classroom management—United States. 2. Self-management
(Psychology)—Study and teaching—United States. 3. Effective
teaching—United States. I. Title.
   LB3013 .C84 2000
   371.102'4—dc21   00-010209

06 05 04 03 02 01   10 9 8 7 6 5 4 3 2

WINNING STRATEGIES for Classroom Management

105301

Acknowledgments

The ideas presented in this book are a compilation of strategies I've observed in the 35,000 classrooms I've visited as a teacher educator. Whenever possible, I've given credit to the teacher who developed the idea. If I have left out a name, please let me know so that I can give proper credit in the future.

Special thanks go out to the teachers who have participated in the Raising Healthy Children Project, University of Washington. Those teachers in elementary and middle schools in the Edmonds, Washington, School District welcomed researchers into their classrooms as we studied the effects of effective teaching strategies on student behaviors. This book is about those effective kinds of teaching behavior: connecting and bonding to students, teaching students self-management skills, integrating the goals of self-management into the curriculum, and finding the causes of misbehavior.

Seeking Self-Discipline

S tandards tell us where we're going—what students should learn. They don't tell us *how* to get there. In particular, what experiences or factors, in and out of the classroom, can help students achieve these standards? This question was addressed in a meta-analysis of 50 years of research, looking at 11,000 statistical findings and 28 factors (Wang, Haertel, & Walberg, 1994). The findings conclude that classroom management has the greatest effect on student learning, as compared with other factors including cognitive processes, home environment and parental support, school culture, curriculum design, and school demographics. It seems only logical, therefore, that as we prepare students for the standards of the 21st century, we examine classroom management. This chapter examines

- How discipline relates to standards
- How changing classrooms (e.g., increases in poverty level students, diversity, inclusion) demand better management strategies
- How format changes (e.g., multi-age classes, looping, blocking) increase the need for better management
- The similarity between effective parenting styles and effective management styles
- The similarity between what skills employers demand and the self-management skills taught in an effectively managed classroom

Other chapters discuss how we can connect to students and arrange our schedules, classrooms, and schools to best serve their needs while encouraging students to build self-esteem and to learn to motivate themselves.

Discipline and Standards

When parents and teachers are asked to generate synonyms for classroom management, discipline is always listed. For our purposes, discipline is "to teach" students self-control, not "to punish." In fact, punishment as a form of discipline to gain control is a last resort. Our goal is to establish a community of learners who feel bonded and connected; such a community exhibits self-discipline and perseverance and takes responsibility for learning.

The greatest sign of success for a teacher . . . is to be able to say, "The children are now working as if I did not exist."

—*Maria Montessori*

Now you may be wondering if taking time to discipline, to teach self-control, is at odds with teaching to standards. After all, there are only so many hours in the school day and the number of standards keeps growing. The importance of time on task has been heralded since the publication of *A Nation at Risk: The Imperative for Educational Reform* (National Commission on Education, 1983). The not-so-surprising finding that "the more time students spend on task, the more likely they are to master that task" seems to dictate that we should devote our time to the standards, not to teaching self-control. For the spectator from an ivory tower, this might be the case. For the teachers in the trenches, we know better.

Imagine that a teacher allocates a considerable amount of time to teach to a standard that requires students to investigate a topic and write a research report. That standard requires that students organize their time, perhaps participate as a member of a small group, stay focused over a period of time, and to self-monitor their progress. What happens when students don't have these skills? Teachers may find themselves nagging the reluctant learners, intervening when misbehavior interrupts group work, and then perhaps resorting to punishment. All of this takes time away from teaching and learning and creates an unpleasant tone in the classroom, which is felt by all students. The reality is that time spent preparing students with the skills for learning purchases more time on task than directly pursuing standards.

The approach to classroom management that I'm advocating is proactive: Teachers need to anticipate what skills and work habits students need so that they can demonstrate high levels of performance on state and national standards. The proactive teacher teaches self-control first—before content standards.

As we prepare students for the future, we need to look at the standards. Most standards require work that extends over a longer period of time than the behavioral objectives of the past, which may have been measured in less than a day. On top of this, many secondary schools have moved to block scheduling, using a 90-minute or longer class period instead of a 48-minute period. Block scheduling requires a learner to stay focused over a period of time, schedule or allocate time, and be self-motivated.

Don't make excuses— make good.
—*ELBERT HUBBARD, PUBLISHER, EDITOR, AND WRITER*

Although in the past assessment was largely based on paper-and-pencil test scores, today's students can demonstrate their learning in many ways. As they make a choice to use Hyperstudio software, keep a diary, or prepare a scrapbook for their project, they demonstrate self-awareness of their interests and talents. As a result of their decision, assessment forms may include using scoring guides (rubrics), measuring group work, evaluating problem-solving skills, rating project presentations, as well as valuing the quality of the ideas. Having multiple forms of assessment available requires that a learner be able to problem solve both in and out of a group and exhibit prosocial, or interpersonal, skills. Both students and teachers use scoring guides to evaluate student work. Using scoring guides and giving effective feedback is an additional form of assessment, which requires an empathic individual who can sense feelings and perspectives of fellow students.

How Classrooms Have Changed

Classrooms have changed over the last several decades. We have more children living in poverty. With inclusion, we have students who used to be educated in self-contained classrooms included in mainstream classrooms. We have more students with clinical depression or with uncontrolled anger. On top of all of this, we have increased accountability for meeting standards. Pressure is felt by students themselves. Some states are doing away with social promotion. Students must meet standards, or they'll face another year in the same grade.

Diversity

Some educators have compared the diversity of today's classroom with teaching in a one-room schoolhouse in the middle of the 19th century. The comparison, however, doesn't do justice to the range of diversity. Students in the one-room schoolhouse differed primarily academically. In today's classroom, student diversity has increased academically, emotionally, and socially. Add to this the increase in non-English-speaking students, students from different cultures, and students with physical disabilities—now you've got true diversity. Increased diversity has greatly increased the need for improvement in classroom management if we are to meet the needs of all students.

Just look at the diversity in classrooms. The Carnegie Foundation (summarized by Fuchs, Fuchs, Mathes, & Simmons, 1997) reported that 26 percent of children in the United States had limited English proficiency and that 24 percent were immigrants. In 1970, 21 percent of schools were minority. In 1992, 40 percent

When one door closes, another door opens; but we often look so long and so regretfully on the closed door that we don't see the ones which open for us.

—ALEXANDER GRAHAM BELL

of schools nationwide were minority. Less than half of U.S. teachers feel sufficiently trained to meet the needs of this increased diversity (National Center for Educational Statistics, 1999).

Can you just imagine what would happen in a classroom where the teacher simply lectured, expected students to listen, then gave seatwork assignments? This style of teaching, often referred to as data dumping or spraying and praying, was a primary mode of delivery in classrooms in the 1980s. If we want to meet the needs of all learners today, it won't work.

Children Living in Poverty

When we understand our students and their needs, wants, and characteristics, we'll be more effective in designing an environmental fit in the classroom. In *A Framework for Understanding Poverty* (1998), Ruby Payne lists behaviors related to poverty:

Never, never, never, never give up.
—WINSTON CHURCHILL

- Laughs when disciplined; or is disrespectful to the teacher
- Argues loudly with the teacher
- Responds angrily
- Uses inappropriate or vulgar comments
- Fights to survive or uses verbal abuse with other students
- Hands are always on someone else
- Can't follow directions
- Is extremely disorganized
- Talks incessantly
- Cheats or steals

If one out of every four children under the age of 18 in the United States was living in poverty in 1996, then 25 percent (or more) of our students may exhibit these behaviors in the classroom. Instead of viewing these statistics and our students in a negative light, see them as challenges to be met.

Inclusive Education

The increasing diversity of our classrooms hasn't been spread out evenly over the last 100 years or more; rather, most of the changes have occurred during the past 30 years. I'll use inclusive education as an example. Students with disabilities were not in a regular classroom until P.L. 94–142, the Education for All Handicapped Children's Act, passed in 1975 (currently, the Individuals with Disabilities Education Act, IDEA). Even then, students with special needs were included only part time in general education classrooms. By the 1990s, many districts were including mildly and moderately disabled students in the general classroom for most of the school day. Although the law says that children with disabilities placed in a regular education class must be supported with the use of supplementary aids and services, this section of the law has been loosely interpreted.

Little Butte Elementary School in Eagle Point, Oregon, has made inclusion work with a strong collaborative support system in place. Every other week, each teacher collaborates with support teachers (Title 1, Special Education or Resource Teacher and a Child Development Specialist) at a 45-minute meeting. A substitute covers the class while the team meets. Figure 1.1 shows a sample agenda used during these meetings.

During the collaboration, the support personnel give concrete suggestions to the teacher and they share insights as to why certain behaviors are occurring. In addition to participating in these meetings, the support teachers team with the classroom teacher to teach small, flexible groups and to coteach lessons.

Unfortunately, not all schools have found a way to make inclusion work. Sometimes the support person ends up grading papers, fixing bulletin boards, making coffee, and copying worksheets. The trend toward full inclusion versus providing a continuum of services is still being debated (ASCD *Curriculum Update*, 1994).

Don't ever take a fence down until you know the reason why it was put up.

—G<small>ILBERT</small> K<small>EITH</small> C<small>HESTERTON</small>

⚸ **Figure 1.1**
AGENDA FOR COLLABORATIVE SUPPORT SYSTEM

1. 60 seconds of successes *(teacher shares)*
2. Any items you would like to discuss *(teacher identifies)*
3. Student review *(collaboration)*
   - new students
   - special-needs students (e.g., those who speak English as a second language, have learning disabilities, or have attention deficit disorder)
   - behavior concerns
   - other
4. Reading, writing, and math benchmarks

Some argue that the inclusive education model has left average students to fall through the cracks (see Ratnesar, 1998). Whatever the outcome, we have special-needs children in our classrooms and we need to adapt the environment to fit their needs.

How Format Has Changed

The format of schools has changed. For example, few of today's teachers stand in front of a graded classroom of children for nine months, in one hour blocks. With the increasing diversity of students in our classrooms, we have transformed the school day. The resulting format changes only increase the demand for better classroom management.

Multi-Age Classrooms. A popular way of restructuring elementary classrooms in the 1990s was to establish multi-age rooms, with students from two or more grades staying with the same teacher for two or more years. The rationale for this structure was to provide a more individualized approach to teaching, more time for teacher-student bonding, and opportunities for cross-age tutoring. In his review of the research on multi-age classrooms, Veenman (1995)

A journey of a thousand miles must begin with a single step.

—*Lao-Tsu*

found that student learning in a multi-age setting does not differ from learning in single-grade classrooms. In fact, Gutierrez and Slavin (1992) found that achievement goes down in nongraded classrooms which have more individualized instruction, less teacher-directed teaching, and more seatwork. Based on their finding of a small negative effect in their analysis of multi-age classes, Mason and Burns (1996) point out the difficulty in management when multi-age classroom teachers must deliver two different curricula to students of twice the age range in the same amount of time as teachers in a regularly graded classroom. What all of the reviews point out is that classroom management is a key factor if multi-age classrooms are to be successful. The power of reviewing the research is that the information helps us to understand what not to do as well as what strategies are important for success.

Looping. In the last half of the 1990s, many elementary schools moved from an emphasis on multi-age classrooms to looping, which is a single-grade class with the same teacher for two or more years. The argument that supports looping is an increased opportunity for teachers to bond with students and the continuous progress of students from one year to the next. In this case, classroom management should be easier because returning students already know the rules of the game. (A similar case can be made for the multi-age classroom.) A cautionary note, however, is sounded by Sanders (as reported in Pipho, 1998). Sanders found that the single largest factor affecting academic growth is the difference in the effectiveness of individual classroom teachers—the effects being both cumulative and additive. While a strong teacher who exacts learning gains from a student has a lasting effect on that student for the next three years of school (regardless of the effectiveness of the subsequent teachers), a weak teacher also has a negative impact for the next three years.

Block Scheduling. The block scheduling found in middle and

The Winner says, "It may be difficult but it's possible." The Loser says, "It may be possible, but it's too difficult."

—S~OURCE UNKNOWN~

high schools in the 1990s increased the demand for better class-room management. The stand-and-deliver form of teaching simply won't work for 90 minutes. "What am I going to do with the class for 90 minutes?" is a classroom management issue.

Parenting Styles and Management Styles

From parenting research, we know that parenting style can affect a child's success in school (Steinberg, 1996). The authoritative parent is much more successful than an authoritarian or permissive parent. Many people in my generation were brought up with an authoritarian approach: strict rules to be obeyed, a rigid "You'll do it because I told you to" approach. Perhaps in response to such a controlling approach, the next generation produced a lenient or permissive parent who resisted setting limits or responding to disobedience. Although accepting and nurturing, the permissive parent did not set clear goals or make strong demands of a child. Researchers have found that the authoritative parent combines the two approaches, balances nurturing with setting clear limits, gives guidance without controlling, seeks input from children for important decisions, sets high standards of responsibility, and encourages independence, not dependency.

Children have never been good at listening to their parents, but they have never failed to imitate them.

—*JAMES BALDWIN*

It's hard to argue with the premise that we need to develop a caring community in our classrooms—analogous to the permissive parent. Yet, research has found this is not enough. When comparing a caring classroom environment with a classroom that has high aca-demic expectations, the second model is more effective in produc-ing learning (Phillips, 1997). If a teacher spends more time on social-emotional behaviors than on teaching cognitive skills, this finding isn't surprising. The goal is to focus on increasing learning by teaching students the prerequisite behaviors needed to meet standards—within an accepting and nurturing environment. Like the authoritative parent, teachers need to balance nurturing with setting clear limits (see Chapters 2 and 3); setting high standards of responsibility, encouraging independence (see Chapter 4), and giving guidance without controlling (see Chapter 6).

Former Army general and Seattle Schools' Superintendent John Stanford believed there is a common ingredient in successful generals, parents, and teachers:

> Most people don't expect a general to talk about love. But we talk about love all the time, because love is a key leadership principle. Love is what the most famous military commanders use to inspire their troops to risk their lives in battle; it's what the most effective CEOs use to elicit maximum performance from their employees; it's what the best parents use to encourage their children to learn and grow. It's certainly what teachers and principals use to get academic performance from their students (Stanford, 1999, p. 196).

Like so many generals when plans have gone wrong, I could find plenty of excuses, but only one reason—myself.

—WILLIAM SLIM, BRITISH GENERAL

Perhaps Stanford's idea is another way to underscore how important it is to win them over, not to win over them.

Preparing Students for the Work Force

The management skills that we're focusing on in this book complement the skills the U.S. Department of Labor identified as required to find and hold a good job (Secretary's Commission on Achieving Necessary Skills, 1991). If we haven't prepared students to enter the work force, then who will prepare them? This book addresses the following competencies identified in the report: time management, organizational skills, following schedules, participating as a member of a team, listening and responding to verbal messages, self-management (including goal setting and monitoring progress), and taking responsibility.

Goleman found similar competencies required for the job market in the late 1990s: self-awareness, self-regulation, motivation, empathy, and social skills. His analysis of 121 companies with a work force in the millions found that ". . . 2 out of every 3 of the abilities deemed essential for effective performance were emotional competencies" (Goleman, 1998, p. 31). If these competencies are twice as important as cognitive skills, then we must build them into our classrooms. Goleman notes that in studies aimed at identifying why careers are ruined, lack of self-control is a primary factor. Here are other parallels between Goleman's findings of success in the work force and classroom management:

Change done to you is debilitating. Change done by you is exhilarating.

—Source unknown

• A major cause of low performance on the job is frequent distractions. This is also a cause of low performance in the classroom. Seating arrangement, a critical factor in minimizing distractions, are discussed in Chapter 3.

• Employees who feel a sense of helplessness, with little or no choice of how they do their work or with whom, are more likely to be poor performers and have poor physical health. When the supervisor micromanages every step, creativity is suppressed. Perhaps the dishing out of one small assignment at a time—which must be completed before recess or the end of the class period—is an example of overcontrol and micromanagement in the classroom. In Chapter 3 we look at providing work menus for students, menus that allow for choice and put students in control of managing their time.

• Top performers have a passion for feedback—how well they are doing. They seek this feedback when it is most useful to them—when they can adjust their performance. In Chapter 2 we discuss how to seek feedback from students.

• "Listening well is essential for workplace success" (Goleman, 1998, p. 140). Goleman cites U.S. Department of Labor estimates that of the time we spend in communication, 55 percent is spent listening. Active listening, a communication standard found in most districts, is discussed in Chapter 3.

• Setting high expectations for all, then letting employees set their own goals to accomplish these expectations "communicates the belief that employees have the capacity to be the pilot of their destiny, which is a core tenet held by those who take initiative" (Goleman, 1998, p. 150). Many opportunities for student goal setting can be found in Chapter 4.

You have to expect things of yourself before you can do them.

I can accept failure. Everyone fails at something. But I can't accept not trying.

—Michael Jordan

᙭ ᙭ ᙭

Goleman concludes his book with this reminder: "Old ways of doing business no longer work. . . . As business changes, so do the traits needed to survive, let alone excel" (1998, p. 312). Translated to education, Goleman's thought means that old ways of teaching no longer work; as children and our society change, so must our teaching strategies. We are preparing children for a world in which they may be changing jobs every three to five years; where the information explosion in the 20th century was greater than that of the past 2,000 years and promises to be even greater in the next 100 years. The challenge is there—and we can live up to it.

2

Bonding and Connecting

If you would win a man to your cause,
first convince him that you are his sincere friend.

—ABRAHAM LINCOLN

Despite your plan to teach good work habits and prosocial behaviors, your students may not buy into it. Indeed, educators have competition for student attention and habits that didn't exist just a few decades ago. Behaviors modeled by sports and television heroes have desensitized students to violence and antisocial behaviors. I recently attended a professional ice hockey game where a team of 6–8-year-olds played and entertained the spectators at intermission. When several of the youngsters began to fight (similar to what they'd observed the professional players do earlier), the spectators stood and cheered. Try to picture these same students walking into their elementary classroom the next morning and their teachers teaching a lesson on anger management. Why should students value self-control when their heroes on the field— as well as on prime time television—initiate violent acts? How can we compete with the media, video games, and sports figures? Faced with this competition, one almost gets a sense of hopelessness. Can we make a difference?

Yes. The best support for this assertion comes from the American Medical Association and what is perhaps the largest study ever done with adolescents (12,118 adolescents in grades 7–12). Doctors, who are in a reactive stance when they treat the negative health outcomes of adolescence (teenage suicide, homicide, violence, substance abuse, and pregnancy), conducted this study to find out what the protective factors are in homes and schools (Resnick et al., 1997). In essence, this study looked for what can be done to protect adolescents from unhealthy behaviors. The two strongest protective factors were strong emotional attachments to parents and to teachers. Positive relationships with teachers were more important than class size, amount of teacher training, classroom rules, and school policy. When students feel connected to their teachers, fairly treated, and a part of the school, they are less likely to use drugs, drink alcohol, smoke, or have early sex.

If I can stop one heart from breaking, I shall not live in vain; if I can ease one life the aching, or cool one pain, or help one fainting robin unto his nest again, I shall not live in vain.

—EMILY DICKINSON

Ways to Connect with Students

Students need heroes they can look up to—someone to connect with—and that someone can be a teacher. Middle schools tried to encourage connection between staff and students by adding a period for advisory programs. Advisory programs were to help ensure that every child had the opportunity to form a relationship with an educator in the school. While the concept of fostering bonding with an educator during the tumultuous middle school years is sound, the advisory period seems to have "fallen far short of expectations" (Galassi, Gulledge, & Cox, 1997). Another approach aimed at gaining connections in secondary schools is block scheduling, allowing teachers and students to spend more time together (e.g., a 90-minute period), which was to provide more time for bonding and connecting. Yet, simply providing time is not the answer—it's what you do with the time that fosters bonding and creates a caring community.

Taking time to connect with our students, to win them over, is the first step in classroom management. The big question is how to win them over. Deiro (1996, p. 193) studied how teachers form healthy connections with junior high students and identified these strategies:

- Creating one-to-one time with students
- Using appropriate self-disclosure
- Having high expectations with a belief in students' abilities
- Networking with family and friends
- Building a sense of community in the classroom
- Using rituals and traditions

One-to-One Connections. Connecting begins even before school starts in the fall. Many teachers send a postcard to incoming students that welcomes them back to school and into their classroom. A school in Seattle has a picnic in August for parents and students to celebrate the beginning of a new year.

On that first day, greet students as they come through the door with a handshake and words of encouragement. Perhaps put a letter from you on their desks (see Figure 2.1) and attach another sheet of paper, already addressed to you for a response. Not only have you made a connection with each student, but the response is also the year's first writing sample.

The first thing to know about a student is his name. At the secondary level, faced with so many students, you can take a picture of each class that first week of school. Enlarge it and use an overhead marker to write each student's name on the photo. Review the faces and names before each class arrives and test yourself by standing at the door to greet as many students as possible by name.

Cultivate your classroom into a community of learners by making sure students know one another by name, too. One primary teacher asks each student to draw a self-portrait with a name tag, then she tacks them to a bulletin board train called "The 1st Grade Express." She practices reading the names with the class each day and challenges her students to try reading the names by themselves.

Time is the coin of your life. Only you can determine how it will be spent.

—CARL SANDBURG

✒ Figure 2.1
SAMPLE LETTER FROM TEACHER TO STUDENTS

Place an introductory letter on your students' desks to help break the ice and set up a task for the first writing sample of the year.

Dear Students,

      I am looking forward to beginning a great year with you. Let me tell you a little about myself. Then I would like to have you write to me so I can get to know you better.

      Besides a wonderful husband, who is a veterinarian, I have two children and lots of pets. It's nice to have a veterinarian in my home to help care for my two dogs, two cats, and parrot. Do you have any pets at home? Tell me a little about your family, too.

      On the weekends I love to walk the beach. Sometimes, on a cold, wintry day, I just curl up with a book to read as I listen to the sound of the waves. My favorite books are mysteries. Do you have any favorites? How do you like to spend your weekends?

      To help me plan an even more exciting year for you, tell me what you'd like to learn more about. Are there any particular field trips you'd like to take? What kinds of books would you like to read for novel study?

      That's all for now. I am looking forward to reading your letter.

               Sincerely,

               Mrs. Longs

               Mrs. Longs

Use alliteration with older students by having them select an adjective describing themselves, such as Curly Carol or Suave Simon.

To help students get to know each other, collect information about each student and have a mystery person each day. Students guess who the mystery person is as you read three or four clues about the student (e.g., size of family, favorite television program, birthplace, hobby).

Another way to get to know your students is to use a multiple intelligences survey. Begin by using the multiple intelligences identified by Howard Gardner (interpersonal, intrapersonal, musical, linguistic, spatial, bodily-kinesthetic, naturalist, logical-mathematical) and then identify several characteristics of each intelligence. Students can use your characteristics to identify their strengths. An example, adapted from Gardner's work, is shown in Figure 2.2. Think about how much more engaging and motivating you can make the classroom for your students if you have information about them that helps you to nurture their strengths and recognize their weaknesses. Students know you truly care about them as a learner when you use knowledge about them to assist their learning, for example by telling them they can work alone or with a partner, or by allowing them to use headphones to block out extraneous noises while concentrating.

Everyone has an invisible sign hanging from his neck saying, Make Me Feel Important! Never forget this message when working with people.

—MARY KAY ASH

Using Self-Disclosure. Your questions and responses make the class feel that you value their feedback and that you are willing to admit your mistakes and make changes. If you use meaningful dialogue, you may want to write back to some students or comment on the feedback to the whole class. What is important about this process is that the students feel connected to you, the teacher. Deiro (1996, p. 197) defines self-disclosure appropriate for a teacher-student relationship as "the act of sharing and exposing the teachers' own feelings, attitudes, and experiences with students in ways that are helpful to the students." Getting feedback from students and using it to

Winning STRATEGIES for Classroom Management

✦ Figure 2.2
WHO AM I?

Use a multiple intelligences survey to gather information about your students. The information can help you plan lessons to excite and motivate the students.

Direct students to read the statement in the Traits column and to place a ✔ in the column that best describes their assessment and response to the statement.

Traits	Agree	Somewhat Agree	Disagree
I like being alone.			
I prefer to study by myself.			
I am intuitive.			
I like team sports and activities.			
I enjoy working in a small group.			
I have many friends.			
I learn by doing, using my hands.			
I get fidgety if I have to sit and listen.			
I would rather build a circuit than read about it.			
I listen to music while studying.			
I'm aware of sounds in the environment.			
I would enjoy playing a musical instrument.			
Math is easy for me.			
I enjoy strategy games on the computer.			
I enjoy logic puzzles and brain teasers.			
I think with pictures and visual images.			
I like art and viewing movies.			
I doodle and daydream.			
I like to read.			
I enjoy listening to the spoken word (stories, tapes, radio commentary).			
I have a good memory for names, places, dates.			
I enjoy nature and being outdoors.			
I like to categorize plants and animals.			
I notice everyday changes in the environment.			

improve your own teaching creates a climate of trust.

Networking to Build a Community. As mentioned earlier, an adolescent's sense of connectedness to parents and school are the two most important protective factors against a variety of risk behaviors. When a teacher extends the bonding experiences to include parents and family, this partnership undoubtedly strengthens the connections. This is not, however, an easy task. Steinberg (1996, p. 187) found that "one in three parents in America is seriously disengaged from his or her adolescent's life, and, especially, from the adolescent's education." Worse yet, he found only one in five parents consistently attending school programs. It may be valid, then, for teachers to complain that parents aren't involved enough in their child's education. Clever teachers, however, find ways to invite parent participation: invitations to participate, letters home to both parents and students, student-led conferences, monthly assignment calendars, and weekly newsletters are a few examples. Brenda Stingily is a 6th grade teacher in Edmonds, Washington. During the first week of school she begins the connections process by sending home the letter found in Figure 2.3.

Establishing Traditions. Students find comfort and security in traditions and routines. Use routines to establish traditions in your classroom—traditions that can help you connect with students and their families.

• Journals. If students write in their journal daily, try assigning the Friday journal entry as a letter home to a family member. Students can summarize their week at school, what they've learned and accomplished, and goals they set. Students take their journals home for the weekend; the family member receiving the letter writes a response on the back of the page, and the journal is brought back to school on Monday. For busy parents, who spend 10 to 12 hours less each week at home than parents did in 1960, this provides a structured, quality connection with their child.

Treat people as if they were what they ought to be and you help them to become what they are capable of being.

—JOHANN W. VON GOETHE

✂ **Figure 2.3**
PARENT PARTICIPATION

Your child's classroom experience will be as successful and productive as the energy and commitment that goes into it. You may volunteer time in the classroom, help out occasionally on field trips, plan class parties, or come in and introduce special skills or talents to us. We need each of you!

Name _____   Child's name _____

Daytime phone _____   Evening phone _____

❑ **Classroom helper**
   (School day is 9:10 to 3:30—however, before or after school works fine, too.)

❑ **Classroom assistant**
   (tutoring, correcting papers, editing stories, doing research, working on math facts, reading with students, running copies)
      Please circle the day or days you can spend in our classroom:

   M   T   W   Th   F

   Hours most convenient for you _____

❑ **Money collector** (field trips, fundraisers)

❑ **Field-trip chaperone or driver** *(WA State Patrol verification required)*

      morning   afternoon   all day

Volunteer opportunities outside school hours

❑ correcting papers
❑ typing
❑ book order chair
❑ photocopying, laminating
❑ bulletin boards
❑ assembling books and portfolios
❑ organizing parent volunteers
   (phone calls, messages)

❑ planning for outdoor school
   (class camping experience)
❑ planning for 6th grade graduation
   celebration
❑ class parties
   (decorations, games, refreshments)

• Newsletters. Many teachers send home weekly newsletters. It's a bonus if the students write the newsletters, with a small column for the teacher. If you don't have a classroom computer, an efficient way to accomplish this weekly task is to have a template for the newsletter. Each week the columnists write their news on a piece of paper that fits their space in the template, glue it on the master, and it's ready to duplicate.

• Student-led conferences. A higher percentage of parents attend student-led conferences than teacher-led conferences. When students lead the conferences, it also serves to boost student motivation. Students spend a considerable amount of time preparing and selecting portfolio highlights, identifying what they do well, and developing their improvement goals. They may choose to role play the conference with a peer or with the teacher. Figure 2.4 is a simple self-reflection page, which could also serve as a table of contents for the portfolio.

• Homework. Homework does not have to be a solitary activity. Many schools have a homework tradition: Read every night! Students may choose to read to a family member, or the family member may read to them. Figure 2.5 (p. 24–25) is an example of a letter parents might receive to better prepare them for this awesome task of reading with their child.

Early primary students who are establishing study habits, including the habit of doing homework, might take home a monthly reading calendar to be placed on the refrigerator door with a magnet (see Figure 2.6, p. 27). The student crosses off each short activity as he completes it and takes the calendar back to school at the end of each month. The teacher reinforces the three-way connection when she reviews the homework assignment and the student goes home to remind a family member of what they're doing together.

For the teachers who create opportunities for parent involvement yet find limited response, one study may offer comfort. Factors out-

✄ Figure 2.4
SELF-REFLECTION TABLE

As your students prepare for student-led conferences, a simple self-reflection table can help them organize their thoughts and serve as the table of contents for a portfolio.

What is the entry?	Why did I include this entry?	What do I like about the entry?	How could the entry or product be improved?
1			
2			
3			

side the teachers' control may be influencing the parents' decision to participate (Hoover-Dempsey & Sandler, 1997). Some parents may not believe it is their role to become involved in school matters. In addition, parents' sense of efficacy (seeing themselves as capable of making a positive difference) influences their involvement decisions. So don't be too hard on yourself if you don't get 100 percent involvement.

Beginning Meaningful Dialogue

Use the information you've gathered about your students to begin a conversation, a meaningful exchange of ideas. It's much easier to have a meaningful dialogue with students when you know something about them. Glenn and Nelsen (1989, p. 159) warn us about the risk of reducing teacher-student interactions to a multiple-choice exam: Did you? Can you? Do you? Will you? Won't you? Are you? Aren't you? Why can't you ever? How come you never? How many times do I have to tell you? When initiating a conversation with a student, ask yourself

Children are like flowers. If you do not tend them carefully, they will grow wild.

—Source unknown

- Am I asking or telling?
- Would I want someone to say this to me?
- Am I trying to see the student's point of view?

Connecting to students through meaningful dialogue requires time. When will you find the time? You can greet them at the beginning of class and ask, What's been the best part of your day so far? What was the best part of your weekend? Or, at the beginning of class, let students work independently on a written warm-up activity (e.g., a short, practice activity on the board). You determine how many students you'll have to engage each day so that you've systematically talked to everyone by Friday (e.g., 6 students per day in a class of 30). You may decide to adopt the practice of carrying a grade book to note each contact. Questions you ask might be unrelated to school, perhaps about a student's puppy.

⚘ Figure 2.5
READING LETTER TO PARENTS

Use a letter to parents to get them involved in homework and schoolwork. The letter, below, guides parents in how they can help to build their child's reading skills. It shows parents that they are important participants in the education of their child while giving them explicit strategies to use in helping the child.

Dear Parents,

Thank you for taking the time to read with your child. Here are some hints for helping your child improve reading skills:

• Set aside 20 to 30 minutes a day for reading. Your child can read to you when you get home or read to you while you cook dinner. The more time your child spends reading or being read to is directly related to improvement. You may set a kitchen timer to keep track of the time. Try to make your appointment to read the same time every day to establish a tradition.

• Celebrate the number of minutes spent reading at the end of the week. For example, set up a chart to record the number of minutes read each day. Each time you reach 100 minutes, do something special together to celebrate.

• Read WITH your child:

  – Take turns reading. You read one paragraph, your child reads the next.

  – If the book is difficult, use echo reading. You read 2 lines, your child reads them back to you (your echo). This way you provide a model of how the words are read.

  – Give your child a chopstick or a marker (any kind of pointer) to follow along in the book as you read.

❀ Figure 2.5 *(continued)*
READING LETTER TO PARENTS

— Have your young reader find a favorite page in the book and rehearse it until it can be read perfectly. Then let your child perform that page for you. Brag about how well your child read that page to other relatives and friends. Ask your child read that page to them.

— Ask your child to read to a younger sibling. Self-concept for reading improves when a child helps others learn to read.

— Children love break-in reading. You start reading and they can break in and begin to read any time you come to the end of a sentence. You can break in next. Another form of this game is called hot potato: You begin reading and stop at any sentence and say, "Hot Potato!" Your child begins reading and stops at any sentence and says, "Hot Potato, Mom!"

• Read more difficult books to your child. Your child's brain is a "work in progress." Reading aloud helps your child build vocabulary, reading comprehension, listening skills, speaking skills, and writing skills.

Good luck! The ability to read fluently is the most important gift you can give your child.

Thank you,

P. Brice

P. Brice

Another option is to have each student write a ticket to get out the door. A ticket is the student's response to a question that asks for his point of view. How do you do this? Post a question on the chalkboard and ask the students to answer it. Their "ticket" is their written response to you as they leave the classroom. This is a good way to get feedback relative to how connected students feel. Questions might be

- How can I help you be more successful in class?
- What do you like best and least about our class?
- What could I do to make the class more interesting for you?

You can offer students generic sentence starters for writing their tickets:

- I would have liked . . .
- I would like to know more about . . .
- I wish . . .
- I feel . . .
- One thing I'd like to change in this class is . . .

Another option is to ask students to submit tickets in a closed box by the door, thereby assuring anonymity and encouraging honesty.

Sometimes connecting with students requires a little background work, which might include a survey. Blythe and Bradbury (1993) designed an attitude survey for middle school students to measure their perceptions of connectedness to their classroom. The survey included statements related to self-esteem and respect for self and others, as well as short answer questions to prompt students to reveal aspects of the classroom environment that work or don't work for them.

Individual student conferences, including conferences that

*The way to
a man's heart
is through
his opinion.*

—BEN FRANKLIN

✂ Figure 2.6
READING CALENDAR

Use a reading calendar for young students to help them establish homework habits. Make a monthly calendar that displays daily assignments. Ask students to mark off each assignment and return the calendar at the end of each month.

Read labels from kitchen cupboard. How many did you read?	Find a newspaper. How many headings can you read?	Go to a store and read boxes, bottles, cartons, and cans. How many can you read?	List everything at home that starts with the letter *S*. Put the list in a binder.	Next time you're in the car, read billboards and signs. How many can you read?
Make a list of all the foods you've eaten today. Put in your binder.	Open the telephone book. How many things can you read in it?	Write a make-believe story and read it to someone.	Find a magazine you can cut up. Cut out all of the words and phrases you can read and paste them in your binder.	Pick your favorite cartoon from the newspaper. Read it and paste it in your binder.
Take a walk outdoors. Count the number of signs you can read.	Count the number of labels you can read on shoes and clothing in your closet.	Write a letter to someone and mail it. Who did you write to?	Read and copy a recipe of something you like to eat. Put it in your binder.	Make a list of all of the colors you find in your home. Put it in your binder.
Read anything you want to for 10 minutes. What did you read?	Make a list of things that happen in the morning and at night. Put it in your binder.	Find an address book at home. How many names can you read?	Find some junk mail you can read. Paste it in your binder.	Find a cookbook. How many recipes can you read?

spring from writers' workshops, provide a perfect opportunity for a meaningful dialogue. You can begin these conferences by asking students the following questions:

- What did you learn from this experience?
- How might you change it if you were to do it again?
- What do you like best about your writing? Tell me why.
- How did the story affect you?
- What do you want to get better at?

When students request assistance during class, you can start a meaningful dialogue by giving these prompts:

- Tell me how you think you should solve it.
- Talk me through the part you understand.
- I'm interested in your answer. Help me to understand how you got it.
- What do you think is the easiest part about this assignment? the hardest?
- Is this tough? How can I help you?

If you are patient in one moment of anger, you will escape a hundred days of sorrow.

—CHINESE PROVERB

How to Communicate During Strife

When a student starts a power struggle, consider the adverse effect of using a lecture or sarcasm in response. The student has "hooked" you and can escalate the situation. The hostility experienced can create resentment and rebellion, destroying that connection you've worked so hard to establish. A better response is to isolate the student from the rest of the class (the "audience") and begin meaningful dialogue. Curwin and Mendler (1999) recommend starters such as

- I can tell you're feeling upset about this. Tell me what's going through your mind right now.
- Help me to understand what happened. I need to understand

your side of the story.

   • Thank you for trusting me enough to tell me how you feel. When did you start feeling this way?

   • I can see that you are very angry about this. Help me to understand what caused the problem.

   • Let's problem solve together. What do you think we should do about this?

   • Is there anything I could do to help you?

   • I'd like to hear what you think happened. I wasn't there to see it.

Compare the options given by Curwin and Mendler above, and the student's likely responses to these teacher demands:

   • As long as you're in this class, you'll . . .
   • You should be taking more responsibility for . . .
   • I said to do it now!
   • I make the rules here and . . .
   • I don't want to hear about it.

How can a person feel liked, unless somebody likes him? How can a person feel wanted, unless somebody wants him? How can a person feel accepted, unless somebody accepts him?

—ARTHUR W. COMBS, FORMER ASCD PRESIDENT

Noticing Each Student

With most students, bonding and connecting comes naturally. It's a mutual relationship. With some, however, it seems they do everything in their power not to connect—or simply don't have the skills to connect. These are the ones who need it the most.

   The common thread woven throughout all of the school shootings in the last few years is the profile of the student offender: an outsider, an outcast. We can make a difference if we pledge that no student will go unnoticed or unconnected with his teachers. A high school teacher in Idaho (Mizer, 1964) wrote about this commitment when she was asked to speak at the funeral for a student she could only remember as sitting in the last seat of her literature class:

I've never forgotten Cliff Evans nor that resolve. He has been my challenge year after year, class after class. I look up and down the rows carefully each September at the unfamiliar faces. I look for veiled eyes or bodies scrounged into a seat in an alien world. "Look, kids," I say silently, "I may not do anything else for you this year, but not one of you is going to come out of here a nobody. I'll work or fight to the bitter end doing battle with society and the school board, but I won't have one of you coming out of here thinking himself a zero."

꙳   ꙳   ꙳

I don't believe any teacher consciously wants to disconnect from students. Yet, there are everyday events in classrooms that leave students thinking they are zeros. Getting to know each student and taking the time to have a meaningful dialogue with each builds a strong teacher-student connection. Using a warm-up and a ticket out the door routinely establishes a tradition students look forward to. Helping students get to know one another builds classroom community. Networking with parents and families cements the connection. Taking the time to "win them over" establishes bonds that stretch beyond the school year. To paraphrase Henry Adams (1838–1928, U.S. historian): A teacher affects eternity. You can never tell where your influence stops.

How can a person feel he's a person with dignity and integrity unless someone treats him so? And how can a person feel that he's capable, unless he has some success?

—ARTHUR W. COMBS, FORMER ASCD PRESIDENT

Time and Space Matters

Time is the most valuable thing a man can spend.

—DIOGENES

How we use our time and space directly affects student learning. Madeline Hunter, one of my teachers, often said, "Time is the coin of teaching. It's up to us to spend it wisely." There's little argument about the importance of time on task. Besides a tremendous research base in support of time on task, common sense tells us that the more time a student spends on a task, the more likely she is to master the task. In this chapter, we address how to find that time and how much time to delegate to various activities, as well as the following topics:

• The quarter system: teacher talk, whole-group interaction, small-group work, independent work
  • Teaching to the communication standard of active listening
  • Teacher talk and eye contact
  • Classroom distractions
  • Seating arrangement
  • Working independently
  • Working in small groups
  • A balanced approach

The Quarter System

Generally there are four social or task configurations in a classroom: teacher talk or presentation; small-group work; whole-group discussion, and independent work. Our goal is to find a seating arrangement that maximizes the learning opportunity in each configuration and minimizes the time it takes to move from one to another. In addition, we want to promote the skill of active listening, which is a critical component in three of these major social or task configurations. Without active listening, there is no time on task.

Teaching to the Communication Standard: Active Listening

To participate in group discussions, small cooperative group work, or conferences, active listening is required. To learn from direct instruction (teacher talk), active listening is required. In fact, check your state standards under communication skills—you're likely to find active listening listed. See Figure 3.1 to see how the Washington State Commission on Student Learning (1998) describes this essential learning requirement.

Before you can listen to learn, you must first learn to listen.

—SOURCE UNKNOWN

The rubric for this standard provides benchmarks at grades 4, 7, and 10 (Washington State Commission on Student Learning, 1998, p. 41). Look carefully at some of the following benchmarks and ask yourself if the benchmark is easily accomplished when the student is not directly facing the speaker.

- Pay attention while others are talking
- Give evidence of paying attention, such as maintaining eye contact
- Interpret and draw inferences from verbal and nonverbal communication
- Draw inferences based on visual information and people's behaviors

---

✦ **Figure 3.1**
ACTIVE LISTENING STANDARD

The following description of standards regarding active listening is from the state of Washington.

The student uses listening and observation skills to gain understanding.

To meet this learning requirement, the student will

1.1 focus attention
1.2 listen and observe to gain and interpret information
1.3 check for understanding by asking questions and paraphrasing

(Washington State Commission on Student Learning, p. 41, 1998).

You have two ears and one mouth. You need to listen twice as much as you speak.

—Source unknown

Do teachers take more time insisting that students listen rather than assisting with the skill of listening? Take some time to listen to teachers in the faculty room. How many times have you heard comments like, "Oh, these kids today. They spend more time working their mouths than their ears. They just don't listen like they used to." Jane Healy (1990) agrees with this. She has found that children today are less able to effectively listen and process verbal material when compared to children 20 or 30 years ago. The passive listening associated with the 25–28 hours a week children spend in front of the television contributes to the problem.

The constant interruption of commercials precludes active listening. Sitting in front of the TV with a remote control in hand encourages the viewer to switch channels. Listen to student responses in your own classroom. How many times do you hear "Huh?" or "What'd you say?" Could they be switching channels in the classroom, too?

Teaching students how to listen should be taught the first month of school. Students spend more time listening in school each day than any other kind of activity—during teacher talk, whole-group discussion and small-group work. Are they listening or only hearing? When you have music playing in the background, you *hear* it but you may not be paying attention to it. Instead, you might be doing another task at the same time. You can hear without putting your mind to work. It is much more difficult to *listen*. To listen, you must engage your brain.

Although the brain can process between 400–500 words per minute, the teacher talks at a rate of only 120–150 words per minute. The use of the remaining brain power determines the difference between listening and hearing. Listening requires inter-pretation, connecting information to previous knowledge, and constructing meaning.

The curriculum for communication skills includes reading, writing, speaking, and listening, but teachers usually only receive materials to teach reading, writing, and speaking. Listening is often ignored, though direct instruction of listening skills is a necessity.

A great mnemonic to teach older students how to actively listen is FOCUS.

If my eyes you cannot see, don't begin to talk to me.

—*Source unknown*

F = Face the speaker
O = Organize
C = Connect
U = Use questions
S = See pictures

When a student has direct eye contact with the presenter, organizes or chunks what is being said around a topic, connects that information to what he already knows, asks questions as necessary for clarification, and tries to visualize what the teacher is talking about, his mind is less likely to wander or be distracted.

Younger students might learn a poem (Cummings, 1992) to help them remember listening skills:

> Won't you ever listen,
> Listen to me.
> Face to face, eye to eye,
> Knee to knee.

When the teacher needs students to adopt listening positions, the class chorally recites the poem while they adjust their bodies accordingly.

How can you teach students active listening skills? Get them involved in studying listening with activities, such as

• Keeping a log of when they listen to gain understanding, to follow directions, to discriminate environmental sounds (e.g., telephone, siren), and for therapeutic purposes (e.g., their best friend's woes)

• Identifying the consequences of not listening well (in each of the previous categories)

• Listing professions that require good listening skills and the consequences of poor listening (e.g., air traffic controller, waitress)

Poor listening habits can create communication problems. Ask students to make a list of the listening habits of others that irritate them; then ask them to identify which of those habits they might be guilty of themselves. A list of poor listening habits might include

• Dominating the conversation
• Avoiding eye contact, looking around or out the window
• Interrupting
• Doodling, fidgeting, or playing with objects
• Wearing a blank facial expression
• Ridiculing the speaker's ideas

Conversation in the United States is a competitive exercise in which the first person to draw a breath is considered the listener.

—NATHAN MILLER

• Asking a question that requires the speaker to repeat information

Students can rate themselves on their listening habits and then try to imagine how their parents, friends, or teachers would rate them.

Teacher Talk and Eye Contact

Yes, we have to teach active listening because it is a communication standard. In reality, we have to teach active listening because students need those skills as we deliver a short lecture or give directions. Teachers cannot communicate effectively without the first step in active listening: eye contact. Because more than 80 percent of communication is nonverbal, students need to see the person communicating. That is, they should square their body off with the speaker so they are eye-to-eye and knee-to-knee. People retain only about 10 percent of what they hear in a lesson; 20 percent of what they see; but 50 percent of what they both hear and see. When students are not squared off with the teacher, they miss learning opportunities.

Active listening or learning from nonverbal communication includes more than just eye contact. Nonverbal clues can be ascertained by watching hand movements, facial expression, and large body action. These are also the indicators of teacher enthusiasm. Enthusiasm is measured by a teacher's use of eyes, hand movements, large body movements, choice of words, facial expression, vocal delivery, and overall energy level. In *Enthusiasm Makes the Difference* (Peale, 1967) enthusiasm is described as "aliveness, interest, excitement, zest, vitality, optimistic, cheerful, hopeful." Peale contrasts enthusiasm with words like dull, routinized, desultory, mediocre, purveyor of gloom, apathy, cynicism. He offers sound advice for those who say they don't *feel* enthusiastic: act as you want to be and you will be as you act (p. 28). His advice is supported

Whoever is happy will make others happy, too.

—ANNE FRANK

in later educational research that found that teachers can be trained in enthusiasm (Bettencourt, Gillett, Gall, & Hull, 1983).

Enthusiasm is an important characteristic of effective teachers and it is associated with student learning gains. Goleman (1998) reports that just watching a teacher lecture for 30 seconds can result in assessing the teacher's proficiency with about 80 percent accuracy. And enthusiasm is contagious. We want students to be enthused about the lesson. Teens often say their worst teachers are "dull or boring." Would you even want to engage in active listening if you attended a workshop where the presenter was dull and boring?

Teacher enthusiasm can only enhance the connecting and bonding discussed in Chapter 2. Did you know that the more eye contact you have with your students while you teach, the more likely they are to feel connected and liked? Words are meaningless unless they're backed up by eye contact (Horn, 1997).

If students aren't facing the teacher to make eye-to-eye communication possible, the chance to connect nonverbally with students is lost. Although making eye contact with your students may sound like common sense, why are so many students seated around tables, students facing one another, while the teacher is explaining or giving directions?

Try to withhold judgment as you read the next two sections. Your initial response as we discuss room arrangement for teacher talk may be, "This reminds me of the old days. I thought cooperative learning replaced these traditional seating patterns." Be patient! You may change your mind as we explore how the environment affects listening and learning.

One of the most wonderful things in nature is a glance of the eye; it transcends speech; it is the bodily symbol of identity.

— *RALPH WALDO EMERSON*

Classroom Distractions

What can the teacher do to create an environment that invites active listening? Teacher training has traditionally focused on how to get attention at the beginning of a lesson, but not on how to maintain attention throughout a lesson. Typically, a signal is given (e.g., ringing of a bell or a verbal request for attention) to get a physical attending response. Then the lesson begins with a mental set to engage the student cognitively by hooking in to background knowledge. Yet, in a manner of seconds, this attending behavior may be lost due to competing factors. Although students aren't simply passive receivers of information, we also need to understand that to get attending behavior is a challenge, as Boettinger (1969, p. 28) pointed out long ago.

> Distraction possibility lurks constantly in the minds of the audience, and silently competes for attention with the presentation itself. Impressions from sight, hearing, touch, and smell continually assault the brain for primacy. Subconscious anxieties enjoy additional advantages when the audience is fatigued or preoccupied. Conducting a presentation is much like conducting a battle against a clever enemy: inattention.

What competes for attention in the classroom? The normal distractions are from the following senses:

Hearing. Noises from the hall or playground are obvious distractions and often are not under the classroom teacher's control. Noises within the classroom include the overhead projector fan, an aquarium pump, conversations among students, or just plain fidgeting noises.

Touch. Imagine sitting in a chair that's too small for you (or too large). Feelings of discomfort interfere with listening. So, too, are feelings of being too hot or too cold. Even young children who come to a carpeted area for many lessons are distracted by touch (sitting too close to one another). Masking tape on the floor can assist with placement of students in rows, which can keep them from touching each other. One teacher rotates her rows each day of the week so that everyone has a chance to be in the front once a week (and only has to be in the back row once a week).

Sight. Animate or inanimate scenes outside the windows lure eyes away from the speaker. Clutter or visual chaos may have the same effect: fluttering mobiles or brightly colored graphics on every inch of wall space compete for attention. Perhaps the worst example of sight distraction I've encountered was the classroom that had students seated around tables and a small animal cage (with a hamster, gerbil, or rat) in the center of each.

Another aspect of distraction is the quality of the visuals the teacher is using. Using overhead transparencies with small type that render the information difficult to read turns off even highly motivated learners. In contrast, pleasing graphics with appropriate color give students something to focus on and provide novelty for the students who are easily bored.

Seating Arrangement

The most widespread instance of visual distraction occurs in the classroom where students are seated around tables looking at one another during teacher talk. Four of the five senses are distracted: sight, hearing, smell, and touch. Thoughts about what that person across the table is wearing or doing compete with the teacher. Placing students with distractibility problems around tables all day only exacerbates their problems. In fact, students diagnosed with ADD should have nothing between them and the teacher during teacher talk. In addition, they should not be seated close to other students with distractibility or hyperactive symptoms. Neutralizing the distractions in the classroom is a necessity if we are to get active listening and not just hearing from all students

The use of space and room arrangement has a direct effect on time on task. How should the tables or chairs be arranged? Figure

3.2 shows four possible configurations. The seating pattern should both maximize the opportunity to focus on a task and actively listen, as well as minimize transition time between activities. Competing distractions must be minimized during teacher talk. The transition from teacher talk to small-group work or independent work should take only seconds.

Working Independently

Imagine that you need to sit down and plan your family budget or to write a letter to an ailing friend. Would you invite a few friends over, to sit around a table with you while you work on these tasks? Or, you are well into a best-selling novel. Would you select a group setting to continue your reading? If you're like most of us, you'd seek solitude to concentrate on these tasks.

I recall when speakers on cooperative learning encouraged teachers to use cooperative groups most of the day. Unfortunately, many teachers unthinkingly took this advice and arranged their students' seats into groups. Ironically, the teachers separate the students when it is time to take the test!

When and why is it important for students to work alone? Let's look first at what the work force demands. From the SCANS report of what the work force expects from high school graduates (Secretary's Commission on Achieving Necessary Skills, 1991), many of the basic skills, higher-order thinking skills, and personal qualities are practiced in an independent setting: writing letters, manuals or reports; reading technical materials or schedules; performing basic computations; taking responsibility; persevering toward goal attainment. Many state and district standards are designed for independent work. The student is expected to

- read at least 25 books each year
- produce a narrative account; a report; a reflective essay

✄ Figure 3.2
SAMPLE SEATING ARRANGEMENTS FOR THE CLASSROOM

Choose the best seating arrangement for your students, depending on the task and their needs while learning.

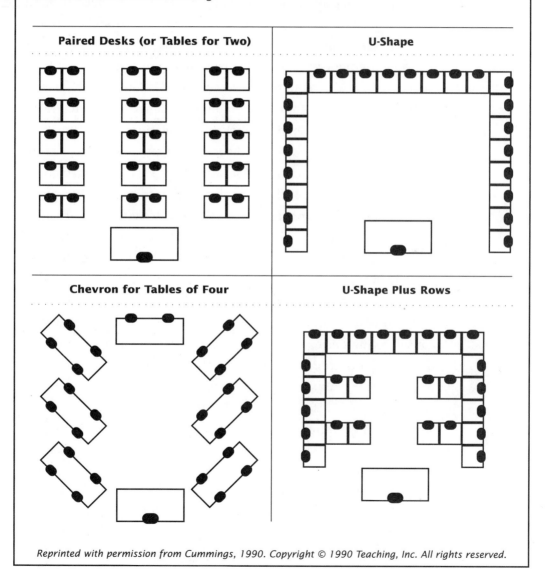

| Paired Desks (or Tables for Two) | U-Shape |
| Chevron for Tables of Four | U-Shape Plus Rows |

- demonstrate rules of the English language in written work
- demonstrate understanding of numbers and operation concepts, geometry, measurement concepts, algebra concepts

Just look at how we assess student learning. Do students take their tests in a small group or alone? Yet, despite the need to learn and practice these skills independently, many classrooms have students seated in small groups the entire day.

What are the potential problems of being seated around a table, in close physical proximity to other students? Many of the same factors that compete for attention during teacher talk are distracting students during independent work: sight, hearing, touch, smell. Students with attention deficit disorder will experience more problems in this seating configuration when they are expected to concentrate on a task. With short attention spans, distractibility, and hyperactivity, they are most likely to focus on things that are novel, highly stimulating. or interesting (Amen, 1998). The odds are that the other students around the table exhibit more of these characteristics than the teacher's independent assignment.

Whether a teacher prefers to have tables or feels stuck with tables, it is our professional responsibility to *assist* students with concentrating during independent work. Amen reminds us that many students are not "off task" by choice; rather they have a prefrontal cortex malfunction that causes distractibility and impulse control problems. He points out that the more a student is pressured to concentrate and work, the less effective the student becomes. Instead, teachers need to create an environment that limits the distractions, lowers the level of concern, and provide work that the student finds interesting. Create a private office or study carrel by connecting two manila folders together so they provide a freestanding, three-walled enclosure for a desktop. This enclosure helps minimize visual distractions. Headphones help muffle environmental noises. Having clipboards available so students can take their work to other quiet places in the classroom may improve concentration.

Providing Choice. One of the best ways to assist students with independent work is to introduce the element of choice. Have you ever wondered why so many students can persevere at a computer game or be glued to a comic book for an indefinite period of time, yet these same students are easily bored and distracted during a classroom assignment? In fact, they seldom finish any task. Change forced upon students is debilitating; change chosen by students is exhilarating. The exhilaration or inspiration produced by making a choice can sustain students through their tasks. For independent work, choice can include the elements of both time and task. Traditionally, teachers have given one assignment at a time and a time limit within which to complete it. Many students have trouble sustaining attention with this one task and find themselves daydreaming or bored; therefore they intrude into another student's work space and do not finish their work.

A menu of activities provides a great opportunity to break the old paradigm of giving all students the same task at the same time and giving all students the same amount of time to finish. If you believe that all kids can learn, but not on the same day and in the same way (Spady & Marshall, 1991), then a menu will help you adjust both time and style of performance. It starts with the main dish—that is, the activities that are required for all students (yet students can do them in any sequence, providing an element of choice). The side dishes include tasks that offer extensions to the unit and reflect the multiple intelligences. Students might be required to complete three of six side dishes, and they get to choose which three. The dessert portion of a menu usually includes related activities for which no product is required; they are enriching and optional. Both side dishes and optional dessert portions may be set up as learning centers around the classrooms.

Not only will a menu provide for a greater range of activities, it provides opportunities for you to differentiate on the basis of student interest. The menu activities may be completed in one to four weeks, depending on the complexity of the activities. This extended period of time, compared with a homework assignment due in 24 hours, provides practice in the applied learning standards of decision making and time management. It also provides the opportunity to layer the levels of investigation of a topic, leading the way to deeper levels of understanding.

Figure 3.3 illustrates the basic structure of a menu. A menu in a social studies unit on social problems (adapted from Burke, 1993) is shown in Figure 3.4. Figure 3.5 is a simpler menu, for younger children involved in a fairy tale unit.

When you design a menu, include the assignments that you would have given during the unit. The only thing that is routine is the time you provide each day to work toward menu completion.

Let's look at young students working on the Fantasyland Menu (Figure 3.5) for 30 minutes each day. Jason, with a short attention span, may spend part of that time writing his sentences and then move on to work on his story map. Kellan, who is feeling very stressed and angry, chooses to go to the listening post. He'll go back to his fairy tale another day. Tonda, who takes twice the time to finish any assignment because she is often off task, uses her two weeks on the main and side dishes. If you support the belief that there is nothing so unequal as the equal treatment of unequals, then you also support the use of menus in the classroom.

I use not only all the brains I have, but all I can borrow.

—WOODROW WILSON

Small-Group Work

Small, cooperative group learning is an important component of an effective classroom when it is balanced with the components of working alone, teacher talk, and whole-group interaction. Yet, just

✄ **Figure 3.3**
MENU PLANNER

Use this template to help you plan a menu for your classroom.
See Figure 3.4 for a complete menu.

Menu: _____

Due: All items in the main dish and the specified number of side dishes must be complete by the due date. You may select among the side dishes and you may decide to do some of the dessert items, as well.

- -

Main Dish *(complete all)*

1.

2.

3.

4.

- -

Side Dish *(select _____)*

1.

2.

3.

4.

- -

Dessert *(optional)*

1.

2.

3.

✂ **Figure 3.4**
SAMPLE MENU

Use a sample menu of projects and activities to give students choices in how
they work and learn about a unit of study.

Menu: Social Problems
Due: 1 month

Main Dish (*complete all*)
❏ Summarize two articles (of your choice) on your subject.
❏ Interview two original sources
   – Develop a survey or questionnaire for the interview
   – Develop a problem-solving matrix
❏ Design graphics to highlight three main points.
❏ Prepare (type) a 10-page report with your proposed solutions.
❏ Present your report orally to a panel of experts.
❏ Write a letter to a person or agency of your choice presenting your proposal.
   Use your powers of persuasion.

Side Dish (*select two*)
❏ Video corner: View the video on interview techniques. Take notes; apply to
   your main dish (interviewing sources).
❏ Volunteer one hour at a social agency.
❏ Music center: Here are both taped and written lyrics with reference to social
   problems. Prepare a one-page opinion or reaction paper to one song. Or, if
   you prefer, select a song of your choice that relates to the social problem you
   are tackling.
❏ News center: From the news journals and newspapers at this table, cut
   out articles related to social problems. Add them to the class mural on social
   problems.

Dessert (*optional*)
❏ Read a novel of your choice connected to real-life social problems. (A list
   of possibilities is attached.)
❏ Write your own music or lyrics to highlight the social problem you selected.
   You can record the music on a class tape or submit the lyrics in writing.
❏ Prepare a poster to increase public awareness of your social problem.

Adapted from Burke, 1993

**✈ Figure 3.5
SAMPLE ITINERARY**

Destination: Fantasyland
Due: 2 weeks

- -

Main Trip *(Complete all)*
❑ *Select one fairy tale.* Read it
　　○ to yourself.
　　○ to one other person ＿＿＿＿＿＿＿＿＿＿＿＿＿＿＿＿＿ .(name)
❑ *Complete a story map* (to show characters; setting; problem; solution).
❑ *Find five new, interesting words.* Write a sentence for each word.

- -

Side Trips —Learning Centers *(Choose 1 or more)*
❑ *Comparing center:* Compare this fairy tale to another story you have read.
　How are they alike? How are they different? Choose your design: trifold, flip
　book, or mini-book.
❑ *Tape center:* Record your favorite part of the fairy tale on the recorder.
❑ *Art center:* Illustrate the most important event in your fairy tale.

- -

Rest Stops
❑ *Listening post:* Listen to a fairy tale tape of your choice.
　　Title: ＿＿＿＿＿＿＿＿＿＿＿＿＿＿＿＿＿＿＿＿＿＿＿＿＿＿＿＿
❑ *Library corner:* Find another fairy tale to read.
　　Title: ＿＿＿＿＿＿＿＿＿＿＿＿＿＿＿＿＿＿＿＿＿＿＿＿＿＿＿＿

having students work in small groups on a question and telling them to be prepared to share their group's thinking or answer is not sufficient. More often than not, the high achiever will do the work while the others go along for the ride. To have positive effects on achievement, cooperative learning groups must have group goals and individual accountability (Stevens & Slavin, 1995). If a group product is involved, each student receives a grade relative to his own work—not a team grade. In fact, if the cooperative task involves a problem with an ill-structured solution and group interaction is limited to just giving answers—with no explanation—achievement goes down (Cohen, 1994).

A more structured group activity is required. Structure can be added with techniques like these:

• Numbering off in the group—participation is determined by numerical order.

• Dividing up the tasks equally, with each student responsible for a certain part.

• Keeping group size to a minimum.

• Assigning roles that require detailed explanations. For example, in literature circles, the discussion director not only asks questions but describes the kind of question: "This question is inferential. What do you think will happen next?"

Pairs are the simplest cooperative grouping to organize. When the pair is heterogeneous—with one student more academically talented than the other—peer tutoring occurs. Significant reading gains were made in one study (Fuchs et al., 1997) where the control group of students used three structures for partner reading:

1. Partner reading with retell (stronger reader reads first for 5 minutes; weaker reader rereads same passage)

2. Paragraph summary (read one paragraph at a time and identify subject and main idea; readers take turns)

3. Prediction relay (make a prediction of what's on the next page; read; then confirm prediction; predict next page, and continue the process for 5 minutes. Then switch roles and continue as time allows, either through a chapter or throughout the book.)

Strategy 1, with repeated readings, improves fluency for students.

Strategies 2 and 3 have taken the processing strategy expert readers already use and by turning it into a read aloud, made it an

instructional strategy for less accomplished readers. Highly structured cooperative activities like this provide the necessary assistance to effectively mainstream academically handicapped students.

My dream of the ideal classroom would be to have team stations
scattered about the classroom with whiteboards or chart stands for
each team. For independent work, students may remain at their
desks; for group work they assemble at their station. For accountability, they might each have a different colored pen, signing their
contribution with their own pen. Different colors makes it easier for
the teacher to monitor individual work and for students to share
work with one another. When you want students to analyze different
charts, have groups rotate around the room to visit the other stations. Hold them accountable for thinking by asking for a written
response on each chart. For example, if teams were asked to list the
major factors that might influence population change in a country,
visiting teams might be asked to circle any factors on the list that
they did not have on their list.

Using a carousel approach to teamwork also gets students up
and moving in groups. For example, after studying the concept of
democracy, hang chart paper on each wall—one for democracy in a
family, in a classroom, in a school, at the city level, and at the
national level. Rotate groups around the charts to add their own
contribution to what democracy would look like in each of these
settings. The activity is similar to musical chairs—classical music is
played while the groups are working; when the music stops, groups
move to the next chart. Again, it's important to set up a traffic pattern by numbering the charts and having groups proceed in numerical order.

Playing the Odds. A primary goal of group work is to get students actively involved in their learning. The odds are in favor of
this when groups are pairs. At any given moment in time, you have
a 50 percent chance of involvement. When students are working in

trios, you have a one-third chance; in groups of four the odds are reduced to 25 percent. If the groups get any larger, "hitchhiking" (simply going along for the ride) becomes an even greater reality. You want teams of three or four, however, for certain activities. For example, in brainstorming you want as many different ideas as possible—four heads are better than two. Or, for longer projects that require a division of labor, larger groups may be more effective. If we are to prepare students for the world of work, they need opportunity to participate in self-managed work teams. Goleman (1998, p. 219) points out: "By the 1990s, teamwork became the most frequently valued managerial competence in studies of organizations around the world."

Balance Is Best

Too much of the same thing is boring! The quarter system guides us in planning how to spend time in the classroom, providing a balance among teacher talk, whole-group activities, small-group work and independent work.

Perhaps a sense of confusion emerged as a result of the strong research in the 1980s favoring direct instruction from teachers as more effective than seatwork. This was interpreted by some to mean that teaching students as a whole group was best. Imagine teaching a directed reading lesson to a class that ranges from nonreaders to fluent readers. It doesn't have to be an exclusive situation. A combination of direct instruction *in a small, homogeneous group* while the remainder of the class is in cooperative groups or working independently has a positive achievement effect in a nongraded classroom (Gutierrez & Slavin, 1992). The prerequisite to this is that students at their desks have the skills to work without direct teacher supervision.

The Material World is a project given to middle school students (adapted by Sarah Treworgy, Alderwood Middle School in Edmonds,

Washington). It provides an example of a creative combination of the quarter system. Short lectures and discussions focused on the differences between developing countries and more advanced countries. Working in pairs, each team selected a developing country and a highly industrialized country to compare. Each partner took a different country to research. Students had a research grid (with questions about government, religion, rights, population data, and environment) to standardize their reports. Then they developed a visual display. When the visual comparisons were completed and displayed in the classroom, students were given a "walk-around test," where they could walk around the room to locate answers for the test from the displays.

Instead of asking students to review for tests independently or in a small group, try a walk-around review. Give them a sheet of test questions and ask them to find someone in the class who can answer each question. The goal is to have as many names as possible, not the same name for each answer (see Figure 3.6).

The creative blend of social configurations can be a choice, as well. During reading, for example, give students a choice of reading independently, taking turns reading in their small group or with a partner, or listening to the teacher reading the same novel aloud. Provide these choices after a direct instruction lesson or watching a movie. Students may either reflect on their learning in a journal (independently), in a small group, or with a teacher-led group. In my classroom visits, I've watched the students vary their choice from day to day—intuitively seeking novelty.

The model shown in Figure 3.7 (p. 53) is helpful in planning and analyzing your use of time in the classroom. What does this look like? Figure 3.8 (p. 55) is a model of a lesson that took about 90 minutes. At the end of a unit on persuasive writing, a class of middle schoolers was asked to write a persuasive essay with the prompt: Is it OK to tell a lie? In preparation, students had to think

Figure 3.6
WALKING REVIEW

Here's a sample of a walking review exercise that gets students out of their seats and encourages them to mingle while learning.

Directions: Find a classmate who can answer one of these questions. Write the classmate's name in the box along with the answer to the question. The goal is to find the answer to each question AND to have a different person's name in each box.

1 Give one example of imperialism. Name.	**2** Why was China in the late 1800s unable to defend herself against aggression? Name. . . . .
3 Compare the Monroe Doctrine and the Open Door policy. Name.	**4** How did the Immigration Act of 1924 affect the United States? Name. . . . .
5 Contrast the U.S. position on neutral rights in Napoleonic wars, World War I, and World War II. Name.	**6** Why was Hitler able to rise to power in Germany? Name. . . . .

✁ Figure 3.7
HOW TO DESIGN A LESSON WITH STANDARDS

Standard: Begin your planning with the "end" (the standard) in mind. Break the learning into chunks; that is, meaningful bits of information that can be developed in 10–15 minutes.

Input: Plan how students will acquire the information or skill. Use the quarter system as a guide. "Teacher talk" for direct instruction includes movies and guest speakers. If the lesson is to be accomplished through inquiry, try small group, independent work, and Socratic style (whole group questioning).

Processing: Students need time to process the information. Can students do this alone or in their small group?

Time: How much time will you spend on each chunk? Do you have 48 minutes (the traditional secondary class period) or 90 minutes to devote to the overall lesson?

LESSON DESIGN FORMAT

	Standard	Input	Processing	Time
1				
2				
3				
4				

about their immediate response and reasons why they picked that choice. They formed two groups, the "yes" group standing on one side of the room, while the "no" group stood on the other. Throwing a Koosh ball back and forth, the student who caught the ball gave a reason. Then, they worked independently on an essay. When the essays were completed, they worked in small groups to debate their point of view. To ensure that they did not put the other side down, they were not allowed to use the word "but." To encourage equal participation, each student was given five beans—as an idea was given, the student placed a bean in a cup. This lesson creatively includes teacher talk (how to write a persuasive essay), whole-group interaction (taking a stand with the Koosh activity), small-group work (the debate), and independent work (writing the essay).

❧   ❧   ❧

Thomas A. Edison said, "There's a way to do it better—find it!" He also practiced what he preached. Despite many failures, Edison patented more than 1,000 inventions. In response to his failures, he said, "We haven't failed. We now know a thousand things that won't work, so we're that much closer to finding what will." Remember this wisdom as you work to improve active listening in your classroom.

There is no such thing as teaching methods that never fail. Everything is contextual. As we creatively design lessons using the quarter system to spend our time wisely, as we rearrange our classroom environment to minimize distractions and maximize active listening, there are no guarantees! So if your first attempt fails, try, try again.

⚘ Figure 3.8
SAMPLE LESSON DESIGN: PERSUASIVE ESSAY

This lesson design is an example of how you can plan and design your own lessons.

Standard: Students will write a persuasive essay.

Steps to Reach Standard	Input	Processing	Time
1. Review elements of persuasion	Short lecture by the teacher	Whole group: Respond to teacher questions	12 minutes
2. Prewrite	Directions to respond to prompt: Is it OK to tell a lie?	Alone: Brainstorm in journal, responding to prompt	15 minutes
3. Clarify support for your argument and listen to opposing position	Directions for a "wall debate"	Whole group: Students divide into yes or no groups; use Koosh ball to designate speaker	15 minutes
4. Write a one-page argument	Template for writing a persuasive argument passed out	Alone: Write about your position	18 minutes
5. Revise and defend your position	Directions for debate	Small groups: Debate using written argument; must defend position	12 minutes
6. Rewrite and submit		Alone: Write final copy of response to prompt	15 minutes class time; complete as homework

4

Learning to Learn

The ability to learn is an essential skill in this century. Rapidly changing technology has already had an effect on the need to retrain even highly skilled workers. Time management and decision making are essential skills for the 21st century. The question is, then, are we preparing our students for their future? The classroom of the past, in which the teacher choreographed every student activity and gave short assignments with a limited time for completion, can only handicap students who are expected to be members of an entrepreneurial work force.

Secrets to Success

For the past few years a national newspaper, *Investor's Business Daily*, has featured leaders and individuals from all walks of life and shared stories about how they achieved success. Examples from these profiles include Clara Barton and how she founded the Red Cross, P. T. Barnum and how he created "The Greatest Show on Earth," B. F. Skinner and how he developed a new science of behavior, and Leonard Bernstein and his mastery of conducting, composing, and teaching the piano. From extensive research into the lives of these people, the newspaper reveals how they reached success. From the information gleaned, certain traits of successful people

have been identified by the reporters. This chapter focuses on four
of those traits

- How you think is everything.
- Determining true dreams and goals.
- Taking action.
- Being persistent and working hard.

These traits provide a road map to help students learn to learn.
They may, however, provide a challenge for teachers who were
trained in the assertive model (stressing the teacher as authoritarian
enforcer in the classroom). The assertive teacher, humorously
described as the brick wall or the battle-ax, is often depicted saying,
"You'll do it because I told you to." If the students don't follow the
verbal directions to get to work, the assertive teacher backs up the
demands with consequences (finish work on time or no recess). This
reaction ignores the fact that many students don't even begin to
work because they don't have the skills necessary to begin or don't
believe they are capable of doing the work.

Goals are dreams with a deadline.

—BRIAN TRAC

An authoritative or responsive teacher, on the other hand, is
accepting yet firm. Don't confuse authoritative characteristics with
those of being wishy-washy. Teaching students how to learn
requires structure and perseverance from the teacher. And it
requires direct instruction of specific skills, which include time
management and goal setting, as well as an environment where such
skills can be practiced.

If you have read Goleman's *Emotional Intelligence* (1995), you
have noticed the parallels between the secrets to success or traits of
successful people and two of his emotional intelligence characteristics: self-awareness and self-motivation. Goleman's five dimensions
of emotional intelligence are

- *Self-awareness*—knowing your strengths and limitations;
decision-making

- *Handling emotions*—controlling anger, delaying gratification
- *Self-motivation*—a sense of hope and optimism that moves one toward setting and accomplishing goals; persistence and follow-through
  - *Empathy*—the ability to read another person's feelings
  - *Social skills*—the ability to get along with others

Goleman argues that a person's IQ predicts only a small amount of a person's success in life; emotional intelligence predicts 80 percent. We cannot discount the importance of social-emotional learning when we read recent publications on the topic: *Working with Emotional Intelligence* (Goleman, 1998); *Executive EQ* (Cooper & Sawaf, 1996) *How to Raise a Child with a High EQ* (Shapiro, 1997), *Educating for Character* (Lickona, 1991), and a focus issue of *Educational Leadership* (ASCD, May 1997). This chapter focuses on self-awareness and self-motivation; Chapter 6 focuses on the other three emotional intelligence dimensions proposed by Goleman.

In these chapters, you'll find examples for teaching motivation, taking responsibility, and time management at all grade levels. Occurrences of these emotional intelligence skills present the greatest challenge for secondary teachers because the number of students exhibiting these skills declines at the secondary level. In addition, it's not unusual to find that a majority of high school students are disengaged from school and learning. At the high school level, Steinberg (1996, p. 67) found that

- Between one-third and 40 percent of students neither try very hard nor pay attention during class.
  - Two-thirds have cheated on a test during the past year.
  - 90 percent report they've copied someone else's homework.

Learning and doing well are not priorities; the diploma (not learning) is viewed as the main reason for staying in school.

All things are possible to one who believes.

— Saint Bernard of Clairvaux

Although Steinberg looks at the influence of peers and parents in creating this disengagement from school, this chapter focuses on what the teacher can do to increase engaged behavior. In particular, what can the teacher do to motivate students to learn? It is the motivated student who sets goals, perseveres on tasks, and maintains an optimistic attitude despite setbacks.

Self-Efficacy—How You Think Is Everything

Our first task is to convince students they have the capability to perform at high levels. If students expect success, they are more likely to take responsibility for learning (Schunk, 1991). Self-efficacy, the belief that you have the power to accomplish a given task, determines whether a student attempts the task or avoids it. We can increase these expectations for success by

- teaching the skills necessary to perform the task
- teaching goal setting
- encouraging positive self-talk
- breaking long-term projects into small steps
- measuring the success of each small step
- involving students in self-evaluation of their effort

It is never too late to be what you might have been.

—GEORGE ELIOT

Time Management

Can you imagine being asked to set a broken leg when you don't know how to? Yet, we ask students to read a chapter or write a report, and many are missing basic time management and study skills. First, assist students in analyzing how they use their time. Students can use Figure 4.1 to boost their awareness of time management. Ask older students to complete a time awareness log for the week that includes 24 hours. Then direct students to analyze how they spent their time and draw conclusions based on their findings. Include in the analysis how much time is spent socializing

✂ **Figure 4.1**

SAMPLE TIME AWARENESS LOG

Use a log to help your students plan their time and to boost their awareness of how they spend their time. Adjust to 24 hours for older students and to 15 minute increments for about an hour for younger students.

	4:00 pm to 4:30 pm	4:30 pm to 5:00 pm	5:00 pm to 5:30 pm	5:30 pm to 6:00 pm	6:00 pm to 6:30 pm	6:30 pm to 7:00 pm	7:00 pm to 7:30 pm	7:30 pm to 8:00 pm
Sun.								
Mon.								
Tues.								
Wed.								
Thurs.								
Fri.								
Sat.								

with friends, watching television, working at the computer, doing homework, sleeping, studying, pursuing extracurricular activities, and eating.

Students can decide if they're spending their time wisely. After teaching goal setting skills, students can use their time awareness log to set realistic goals. In *How to Raise a Child with a High EQ*, Shapiro (1997) suggests that students take a few minutes each day to list the tasks that need to be accomplished and rank them in order of importance to help develop a plan to manage both time and work. For example, to assist with homework completion, students can list what must be accomplished between 4:00 p.m. and 8:00 p.m. After ranking them by order of importance, determine the amount of time needed to complete each. Students use this checklist the following week, noting which tasks were completed, the actual completion time, and how well they performed the task.

Homework Completion

Homework completion is a worthy goal for students—achievement goes up when students spend more time on homework. Providing both appropriate quantity and quality of the homework, however, is the teacher's responsibility. The recommendation for appropriate time (Cooper, 1994) is 10 minutes per grade. Cooper suggests

- Grades 1–3: 15 minutes on one to three nights per week
- Grades 4–6: 15–45 minutes on two to four nights per week
- Grades 7–9: 45–75 minutes on three to five nights per week
- Grades 10–12: 75–120 minutes on four to five nights per week

Quality can be measured by relevancy and meaning—students aren't likely to be motivated to improve time management if the tasks are boring. In addition, working after school becomes an impediment to completing homework. Achievement in school goes down when high school students spend 20 hours a week or more on a part-time job (Steinberg, 1996), but 80 percent of high school students are likely to have after-school jobs to earn pocket money. The solution to this dilemma must involve the community, parents, and the school.

Informational Reading

Before you can read to learn, you must first learn to read. Many students, however, are missing the skills necessary for reading informational text. Poor readers are apt to try to read a chapter from beginning to end, then wonder why they can't remember what they read. Skilled readers, however, intuitively use a skill called "multipass." They pass through a chapter looking at the organizers before reading the chapter page by page. Organizers include

- Headings
- Subheadings
- Bold print and italics
- Chapter summary
- Pictures and graphics
- Objectives
- Chapter questions
- Vocabulary

Multipass is a skill that needs to be taught and practiced. Knowing that students are most likely to follow the path of least effort, assign activities that require students to pass through the chapter before assigning the chapter itself. Here's a sample set of instructions for your class:

- Read the chapter summary. List three things that you expect to learn from reading the chapter.
- Find one picture you like in the chapter. Make a list of things

you learn from studying the picture alone.

- Outline the chapter using only titles and subtitles.

Study Skills

Before assigning an academic task, ask yourself if there are skills you need to teach first. At the beginning of the school year, basic study skills to teach students include

- Organizing a notebook (3-ring binder)
- Keeping track of work requirements (using an assignment sheet or planner)
- Taking notes
- Test-taking skills (how to prepare for an essay, short-answer, multiple choice, and matching tests)

Highland Park Junior High School in St. Paul, Minnesota, developed an implementation calendar for study skills across the curriculum for the first month of school. Departments were assigned specific skills to teach; for example, the English department taught time management, and the science department taught note taking. Some departments were classified as reinforcement, for each skill—for example, ESL and special education reinforced time management. Other middle schools divide the skills teaching responsibilities among core teams. Some high schools have used the advisor-advisee period to teach skills. Whatever structure works for your school, the students need to be taught the skills necessary to perform successfully in school. When this happens, students can focus their time, be persistent, and work hard.

Nothing happens unless it is first a dream.

—CARL SANDBURG

Goal Setting

When we help students set goals and systematically work at achieving them, self-discipline is heightened. Students learn that they must work hard to get smart.

We all dream. Yet some of us turn dreams into reality. A goal is the building block that turns a dream into reality. All students have dreams—ask them to list the dreams. Then, tell them to work backward until they have identified manageable steps. Model this process with your class. For example, if a student dreams of going to law school, decide what steps must be in place. As she works backward, graduation from college and graduation from high school are two big steps. Work backward until the step is to pass the class the student is in now. Now your student is ready to set goals.

Be prepared with examples of what local universities and employers require for admission or employment because some students may believe that all that is necessary is the high school diploma and that Cs and Ds in classes will not make a difference. For example, some jobs require a writing sample, which may be in the form of writing a persuasive essay telling the employer why she should give the student a job.

Help students to distinguish long-term goals from short-term goals by giving them a list to categorize:

- Getting a high-paying job
- Passing a test on Friday
- Completing the science project
- Graduating from high school

After discussing different types of goals, it's time to direct students to explore the goals.

- Social—I want to have more friends. I want to get along better with my mom.
- Health—I want to get more exercise.
- Academic—I want to improve my math grade. I want to turn in my homework on time.

Give students a chance to write their own short-term goal. They must write one that they really want to achieve and are willing to work for. According to Wilson (1994), effective goals

- Are written in specific, measurable terms
- Can be visualized
- Are achievable
- Are critiqued for potential barriers
- Include benchmarks to measure progress
- Yield rewards that are valuable to the student

Give students a guide to assist them with the process of setting and achieving realistic goals (see Figure 4.2).

Turning Problems into Goals

Goal setting and problem solving are closely connected. For very young students, it is helpful to teach problem solving before goal setting. Very often a goal is a problem you want to solve. For example, wanting to have more friends can be both a goal and a problem. The steps in goal setting may be too abstract for young minds, but brainstorming ways to solve a problem is developmentally appropriate. Just watch a toddler who can't find a toy. He looks in a variety of places and asks a parent for help.

Students can break problem solving into three steps, developing skill in the first step before beginning the second (see Figure 4.3). Each day, identify a problem common to many students: no one plays with me at recess; I didn't get invited to my friend's birthday party; or someone is teasing me. The first step to a solution is to brainstorm as many possible solutions as possible. Be accepting of all suggestions. Step two is to play the "if-then" game. If I choose this solution, then what will happen? For example, young children might suggest grabbing their ball back if a friend takes it. Students learn to say, "If I grab the ball back, then my friend might grab it back again and we'd be in a fight." Step three is to select the solu-

✎ Figure 4.2
GOAL-SETTING TEMPLATE

Students can use this template to help them set and achieve realistic goals.

My goal: _____

ACTION PLAN—Steps to reach my goal:

1.

2.

3.

4.

- I will know I have accomplished my goal by _____ (date).

- Possible interruptions or barriers that may block progress toward my goal include:

- If I need help, I can go to the following people or resources:

- My confidence in reaching my goal is *(circle one number)*

low		mediocre		high
1	2	3	4	5

tion that has the best consequence. When students learn to discriminate win-win from win-lose or lose-lose outcomes, they select a solution that has a win-win consequence.

The best solution to a problem may become a goal for some students. See Figure 4.4 for a sample goal card. For example, if the problem was wanting to make friends, a solution might be saying nice things to others. Give students a goal card on which they

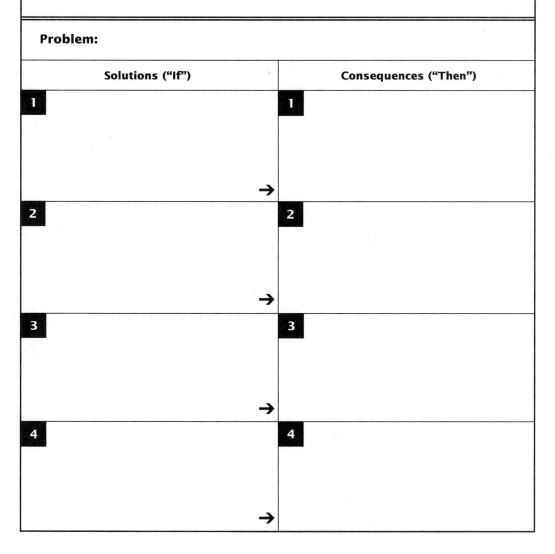

✄ **Figure 4.3**
PROBLEM-SOLVING TEMPLATE

Students can use this format to learn a three-step way of solving problems. Steps are to (1) brainstorm possible solutions, (2) play the "if-then" game (if I choose this solution, then what will happen?), (3) select the solution that has the best consequence (win-win).

Problem:

Solutions ("If")	Consequences ("Then")
1	**1**
2	**2**
3	**3**
4	**4**

record each time they practice their goal. If the whole class is working toward the same goal, the teacher can provide added reinforcement: "I heard Juan give a compliment; Juan, did you color in a point on your goal card?" (Adapted from Cummings, 1993.) Young students collect goals cards to show what social skills they are working on or using.

The goal-setting template (Figure 4.2) can be simplified for younger children:

My goal for today is _____

This is what I plan to do _____

If I need help I will _____

✂ **Figure 4.4**
SAMPLE GOAL CARD

Use goal cards to help your students feel successful.

PUT-UP SCOREBOARD

HOME
(Gave One)

VISITORS
(Got One)

Used with permission. Cummings, 1993

I tried hard to reach my goal.   _____ Yes   _____ No

I made it. _____   I almost made it. _____   I missed it. _____

I didn't reach my goal because _____

You may want to design content specific questions for students to help them set goals. In math, some prompts could be

- Did I finish?
- How many did I get right?
- Am I improving?
- What do I need to work on?
- How many minutes did I work on math this week?
- What is my goal for next week?

If students are assigned "thinking partners," they can talk about their progress toward their goal and help one another with barriers. For students who need extra encouragement to work hard toward a goal, you may have to create a menu of privileges and let a student celebrate goal accomplishment by selecting a privilege. The menu might include being line leader for the day, VIP, sitting by a friend in class for a day, or having his name and the goal accomplished in a newsletter.

Don't forget to model goal setting. Consider writing your personal and professional goals on the board for students to see. Discuss your progress toward them. Let them see what you do when you experience setbacks along the way. Who knows, they may become your best support group!

You must have long-range goals to keep you from being frustrated by short-range failures.

—CHARLES C. NOBLE

Encouraging Positive Self-Talk

How you think is everything! Students who blame others, the task, bad luck, or their own lack of ability, are likely to be quitters. Listen for comments like

- I'm a natural born klutz.
- My teacher doesn't like anything I write.
- You gave me a *D* on my report card.
- This math is too hard to do.

Attributions like these are a signal that the student is placing blame externally and may use excuses to avoid putting effort into tasks. When you hear helpless statements like these, help the student turn the statement into a powerful thought. Instead of "How could I have been so stupid?" try to get the student to say "I can learn from that mistake." A great warm-up assignment when students arrive in class is to post a helpless thought for students to change to a powerful thought.

Remember that you, too, must respond to a student's helpless statement with one that leads back to fostering internal attributions and sense of control over their life:

Student: I didn't have time to read my book.

Teacher: What other choices did you make this morning? What could you do now to get it read?

Student: This math is too hard to do.

Teacher: Let's look at the first problem and do it together. I'll bet you already know most of the steps. I can fill in whatever is missing.

Student: She calls me a name, but I'm the one who gets sent to the office. It's not fair.

Teacher: What happened before she called you a name? When someone calls you a name, what choices do you have? Let's list them and the consequences of each.

Be sensitive to student language. When you hear "I can't" help them rephrase by saying "I don't want to . . ."; "I have to" change to "I want to . . ."; and, "I should . . ." to "I've decided to . . ."

The greatest thing in this world is not so much where we stand as in what direction we are going.

—OLIVER WENDELL HOLMES

Keeping a journal with the theme of "Things That I Can Do" or "I'm a Winner" encourages positive mental messages. Ending each day with a list of accomplishments helps both with continued effort toward goal achievement as well as preparing students for that inquiry at home, "What'd you learn in school today?" Sentence starters like these encourage forward thinking (Edelston, 1993):

Mistakes I made today . . .	What I learned from each . . .
New ideas I had today . . .	What I'll do with them . . .
Problems I had today . . .	How I'll solve them . . .
Positive things I did today . . .	What I learned from each . . .

As your daydreamers look around the room, posted quotes can be motivators to catch their wandering eyes. Change them frequently to add novelty:

If I have lost confidence in myself, I have the universe against me.

—RALPH WALDO EMERSON

- If I think I can . . . I might. If I think I can't . . . I'm right.
- Think win-win (Covey, 1997).
- Shoot for the moon. If you miss it, you'll still land among the stars.
- Winners never quit . . . quitters never win.
- I work hard to get smart.

Classrooms at all grades have used chants and pledges to start their morning. Many upper-grade classes use Marva Collins's (Collins & Tamarkin, 1990) "An Affirming Pledge to Myself"

This day has been given to me fresh and clear. I can either use it or throw it away. I promise myself I shall use this day to its fullest, realizing it can never come back again. I realize this is my life to use or to throw away. I am the only person who has the power to decide what I will be. I make myself what I am.

A rhyme used with younger students (Cummings, 1996) is

What will the day bring? The choice is mine.
It could be bad. It could be fine.
I'll make it win-win, and not lose-lose.
It all depends on what I choose.

With so many things to worry about in our troubled world, we must look for ways to help children maintain that sense of hope and optimism that is critical to success. We must maintain that sense of hope, too. When you find yourself making statements like these, you know it's time for your own self-renewal:

• These kids just aren't motivated.

• When it comes right down to it, I really can't do much about student performance. Their home environment has already determined it.

• I can't do much without parent support.

Whether you believe you can do a thing or not, you are right.

—Henry Ford

Practice reworking your thoughts when you are feeling down. Instead of saying "These kids just can't move from one activity to another," say "I've got to work on my transitions and smooth them out." Make a list of all of the things you do to help students that don't require parent support. Pick up *Chicken Soup for the Teenage Soul* (Canfield, Hansen, & Kirberger, 1997) and read the passages about teachers who have made a difference in the lives of students. Unless we get rid of our negative thinking, it will only continue to infect our students.

Breaking Long-Term Projects into Steps

The high standards being set in districts across the country go far beyond the behavioral objectives written in the 1970s. Products of student learning and performance-based learning require days, if not weeks, to accomplish. For students with poor time management skills and low motivation, these days and weeks might be spent worrying about the task instead of working on it. Procrastination becomes a habit. You can assist students by breaking these projects into small steps.

Begin by making a list of all of the tasks you assign students that require two or more days to complete. Tasks as commonplace as book reports and preparing for a vocabulary or spelling test are difficult for many students who have poor time management skills. Break the task down for students, including benchmark dates indicating when each substep should be complete. For some projects you may include the point value of each small step, see Figure 4.5 for a model.

Checklists help students develop an internal sense of control. Checklists are often content specific, like the model shown in Figure 4.6. At first, teachers may need to monitor the completion of each step and evaluate the quality of the work. Gradually, students are asked to practice this important time-management skill by breaking a task into manageable substeps themselves. The checklists provide scaffolding, a structural support, that is gradually removed as student skills improve.

Step by step. I can't see any other way of accomplishing anything.

—MICHAEL JORDAN

The concept of scaffolding to increase student success can be applied to the length of the project itself. Begin with a three-day or four-day project before working up to a two-week project, which in turn can lead to a four-week project. Begin with projects that include explicit teacher instruction and limited choices before offering students choice of individual projects. The immediate knowledge of results with the shorter project demonstrates to children that effort will pay off in greater success. We want students to recognize that if they try, it will pay off. When effort leads to success, students begin to expect success on future projects. If students do not have strong beliefs in their own capabilities, they may avoid the task altogether.

✂ Figure 4.5
LONG-TERM PROJECT PLANNER

Tasks as commonplace as book reports are difficult for students with poor time management skills. Give these students a planner to help them break any task into substeps. Give points to reward the students for each substep.

Task description:

Substeps	Due Date	✔	Points Possible	Points Earned
1				
2				
3				
4				
5				

✄ **Figure 4.6**
BOOK REPORT CHECKLIST

Checklists offer scaffolding to students who need support in finishing long-range tasks. Teachers can monitor the progress and evaluate the quality of work until the students gradually learn the process of breaking tasks into substeps themselves.

❏ I picked out a book.
❏ I have to read _____pages each day.
❏ I finished the book.
❏ I listed the title, author, and illustrator.
❏ I wrote about story elements (problem, solution, characters, setting).
❏ I wrote my opinion of the book.
Total number of pages in my book: _____
Number of days I have to read my book: _____
Total pages ÷ total number of days = _____ pages per day

Record the number of pages you read each day.

Sun.	Mon.	Tues.	Wed.	Thurs.	Fri.	Sat.

I read my book and finished my report and I feel

_____

_____

_____

The new standards in most districts require culminating projects that may take several weeks to complete. Take time to complete a task analysis of the project and to list the skills necessary for students to successfully complete each task. The task analysis of a culminating project (see Figure 4.7) is adapted from standards set by the Edmonds (Washington) School District for 5th and 6th graders.

This task analysis is then used to guide lesson planning and scheduling. Which skills should be taught directly to students? The task analysis also becomes a checklist to be used by students to guide them through project, as shown in Figure 4.8 (p. 78). Along with this checklist and reflection guide, students receive a rubric describing the criteria to be used in grading the report.

Small Steps for Young Children

Young children need scaffolding to experience success. While the long-term goal may be for students to write in complete sentences, perhaps even to write a paragraph, teachers begin with tiny, discrete steps. The beginning developmental steps include having students

- talk about or describe pictures
- understand that print carries a message
- add words to pictures
- identify the one-to-one correspondence between spoken and written words
- know that print goes from left to right
- copy print

A kindergarten teacher might begin by attaching a picture (e.g., taken from a news magazine) to chart paper each day. Students are asked to name things they see in the picture. The teacher writes the word given by the student, then the student draws a line from the picture to the word. These talking pictures are revisited regularly

✂ Figure 4.7
TASK ANALYSIS OF A CULMINATING PROJECT

The standards in most districts require culminating projects that take several weeks to complete. Take time to complete a task analysis of the project and to list the skills necessary for students to successfully complete each task.

Standard: To make sense out of information gathered from multiple sources and to apply this new understanding to answer a question or solve a problem.

Student Task	Skills Needed
1. Explore the topic	■ How to gather background information ■ How to search the Internet
2. Develop wondering questions	■ How to write good or guiding questions ■ How to determine personal relevancy
3. Select a big question	■ How to sort guiding questions from small, fact-based questions
4. Search resources	■ How to use reference material
5. Make a known list (things the student finds out about the topic)	■ How to identify relevant, congruent information
6. Write three search questions	■ How to use a KWL organizer ■ How to make a web out of information
7. Locate relevant information	■ How to locate information in references
8. Take notes	■ How to paraphrase; summarize; discriminate fact from opinion; make inferences; take notes
9. Organize information	■ How to outline information; use writing process
10. Create and present the product	■ How to prepare charts; create videos; use design elements
11. Evaluate the product	■ How to develop and use a rubric
12. Reflect on the process	■ How to identify growth targets, set goals

Adapted from the Edmonds (Washington) School District standards for 5th and 6th graders

> **Figure 4.8**
> **CHECKLIST FOR RESEARCH**
>
> The information from the task analysis (see Figure 4.7) becomes a checklist to be used by students to guide them through project.
>
> ❏ 1. Topic identified and it is something you are passionate about
> ❏ 2. Internet search completed
> ❏ 3. Guiding questions written
> ❏ 4. Subtopics listed
> ❏ 5. Web done with guiding question as hub; subtopics as spokes
> ❏ 6. Web transferred to outline form
> ❏ 7. Three types of resources located (*Web sites, interviews, museum visits, books*)
> ❏ 8. Notes taken on color-coded cards; sorted by questions
> ❏ 9. First draft written
> ❏ 10. Three visuals or illustrations developed
> ❏ 11. Final draft written
> ❏ 12. Bibliography completed
> ❏ 13. Score yourself on the rubric
> ❏ 14. Reflections guide (below) filled out
>
> **Reflections**
>
> 1. What are the strengths of your piece?
>
> 2. Describe two things you learned about your topic and guiding questions.
>
> 3. What did you learn about writing a research report?
>
> 4. What was especially important or helpful to you as you worked on this project?
>
> 5. If you could continue working on this project, what would you do?
>
> 6. What advice would you give to someone else who was working on a similar project?
>
> *Adapted from Yocum and Tibbits, 1999.*

with students chorally reading back the words (labels). Later these charts are placed at a learning center where students are encouraged to either copy the labels (on strips of paper to encourage printing from left to right) or draw their own picture (like the one on the chart) and add labels (from the chart). Eventually this developmental sequence progresses to selecting a title for the picture, writing an attention-getting sentence for the picture, adding detail sentences, and finally a finishing sentence (see Figure 4.9). It's not unusual to find 1st graders writing paragraphs on their own using a checklist.

Measuring Success and Self-Evaluation

The importance of immediate and specific knowledge regarding student performance is an accepted tenet of good teaching.

It was almost like every minute of every day (I asked myself), "What can I do to improve myself?"

—Bruce Jenner

✂ Figure 4.9
MY TALKING PICTURE PARAGRAPH

Young students (kindergarten or 1st grade) can use this checklist to help them write a paragraph about a picture.

Monday
❑ I selected a picture.
❑ I gave the picture a title (or, wrote the topic).
❑ I wrote an attention-getting sentence using the topic.

Tuesday
❑ I listed three details to support my topic.
❑ I wrote a finishing or "clincher" sentence.

Wednesday
❑ I edited my paragraph.
❑ My study-buddy edited my paragraph.

Thursday
❑ I revised and edited my paragraph.
❑ I published my paragraph by
  __ reading it aloud from the author's chair
  __ reading it to teacher
  __ displaying it on the writers' board

Knowledge of results also helps establish the relationship between effort and success. Too many American-born students believe that their success or failure is fixed by their intelligence—it is out of their control. The strategies in this chapter are to convince them that effort is controllable, and they must work hard to get smart.

Whether students succeed or fail on a task, they are likely to attribute the cause to ability, effort, task difficulty, or luck. By teaching the skills necessary for success on a task, students are shown they have the ability to accomplish the task. Breaking the task into small steps increases the probability of success. Encouraging positive thinking as well as designing your feedback to students to focus on their effort and not their ability encourages internal attributions which are under student control.

Nothing is impossible to the willing mind.

—Books of Han Dynasty

Measuring their success or failure at each small step provides the opportunity for students to experience the consequences of their effort or lack of effort. We must not allow students to use excuses for failure nor should we provide excuses for their lack of success. On the other hand, we need to convince students that success is improvement, not perfection. In this media-oriented world where commercials brainwash adolescents with how to be better and how to look better with certain products, students are exposed to the perspective that "If I don't wear the right brand of tennis shoe, I won't be socially accepted." I worry that we might be sending the same message to students in our classrooms when we post only the *A* papers or ask questions like, "How many of you got 100 percent on your quiz?" The message is, if you didn't get an *A*, you weren't successful. A more effective question would be "How many of you improved from your last quiz?" Letting students select the work to be posted sends a very different message than posting only the best grades.

The spelling agenda shown in Figure 4.10 is an example of breaking a weeklong task into small steps and helps students track their success. Students have a visual model of their improvement (or lack of) as they compare pretest and posttest scores. Each day they practice a research supported spelling strategy to help them improve. The look, say, cover method is better than just writing spelling words several times—students just copy the words. (Spelling is the ability to reproduce a word without a model to copy from.) The missing-word sentence develops understanding of the word because the word is used in a sentence filled with context clues. Students substitute a spelling word for the blank or X. For example, The optical X were created by a trick with mirrors. X = illusions). Their spelling partner must guess which word from the list the X represents. Looking for alternative forms of the same word helps students see patterns in the English language. And, finally, students have a chance for self-reflection on Friday.

Take time for students to reflect on their perseverance in their schoolwork, across assignments and disciplines. Ask them to record where they are now and where they want to be (see Figure 4.11).

Rubrics

The use of a rubric to assess students is increasingly popular. If a scoring guide is given to students before they begin a task, they have the advantage of having the precise description of the criteria used to judge the task. The guide is invaluable as a tool to create internal attributions. That is, a student uses the rubric to self-evaluate the project before turning it in. Instead of shifting the blame for a low grade to the teacher, a student must reflect on personal effort, using the rubric as a guide.

The rubric in Figure 4.12 was given to students along with the assignment for a project and a checklist (Figure 4.8, p. 78). The rubric sets the standard of quality for their work, encouraging self-evaluation, and fostering internal attributions. In addition, it helps students identify that they are in charge of their personal success or failure, not the teacher.

✂ Figure 4.10
MY SPELLING AGENDA

This spelling agenda breaks a weeklong task into small steps and measures success. Students have a visual model to use in comparing their scores on the pretest and post-test. Each day they practice a spelling strategy to help them improve.

Ask students to track their progress by coloring the number of words they get correct on the tests.

	1	2	3	4	5	6	7	8	9	10	11	12	13	14	15	16	17	18	19	20
Monday Pretest																				
Friday Post-test																				

❏ Monday   Self-corrected pretest

❏ Tuesday   Look, Say, Cover
             I own _____ words.

❏ Wednesday I wrote _____ sentences.
             I quizzed my partner.

❏ Thursday   I found _____ alternative word forms.
             I found _____ base words.
             I added _____ prefixes.
             I added _____ suffixes.

❏ Friday   Success is improvement, not perfection.
             ❏ I improved.
             ❏ I did not improve because _____ .

Extra Credit Practice Activities
- Make a crossword puzzle using the words.
- Make a mnemonic (memory trick) to help you remember a word.
- Write a paragraph using your list words; it must make sense!
- Write synonyms for each word.

✄ **Figure 4.11**
SELF-REFLECTION

Use this table and the following scale to measure your success in your
schoolwork and progress toward your goals.
Scale: 1 = seldom; 2 = sometimes; 3 = consistently

SELF-REFLECTION		
Where I am now	**Topic**	**Where I want to be**
1 2 3	I turn my homework in on time.	1 2 3
1 2 3	I use my time wisely in class.	1 2 3
1 2 3	I try hard to produce quality work.	1 2 3
1 2 3	Your choice: I...	1 2 3

Younger children can be given a simplified rubric. A popular one
used in the primary grades is The Three Cs: Complete, Correct, and
Careful Thinking. For Completeness, students decide if their project
is finished, includes extra details, or is not finished. For Correct, the
scale goes from true and new information provided to incorrect or
wrong information. A high score for Careful Thinking includes creative and interesting work; hurry-up work receives a low score. A
three-point scale, instead of the typical four-point scale, is easier for
younger students to use.

Letting young children keep their own log helps them visualize
that their skills are growing. Use your developmental checklist of
skills as a guide that students can fill in when they've mastered a
skill. A portion of a log is shown in Figure 4.13 (p. 86).

✂ Figure 4.12
REPORT SCORING GUIDE

Use a rubric or scoring guide to help set the standard of quality for student work, encourage self-evaluation, and foster internal attributions. Rubrics help students identify that they are in charge of their personal success or failure, not the teacher.

Item	In Progress	Meets Requirements	Goes Beyond Requirements
Guiding questions and topics	Minimal connection to answering guiding question; random collection of facts	Uses acceptable guiding questions and topics	Real world, authentic questions and topics—adds own passion
Research notes	Minimal connection to answering guiding question; random collection of facts	Subtopics address guiding question; notes color coded; includes relevant information	Subtopics add original insight into guiding questions; extensive relevant information on color-coded note cards
Resources	Insufficient resources; lacks variety	Acceptable resources on subtopics	Uses more than five resources; variety; goes beyond actual text; includes substantive conversations and interviews
Writing process	Does not follow writing process	Uses writing process	Excellent use of all steps of writing process

✄ Figure 4.12 *(continued)*
REPORT SCORING GUIDE

Item	In Progress	Meets Requirements	Goes Beyond Requirements
Quality of writing	Guiding questions are weakly addressed or answered in introduction or conclusion; paragraphs not organized or flowing; some data synthesized into own words	Introduction and conclusion address guiding questions; logical paragraphs; subject-specific vocabulary; data synthesized into own words	Introduction shows passion for guiding question; encourages reader to continue; conclusion restates main ideas and connects to guiding question; specialized vocabulary used; data synthesized into original format
Conventions	Does not meet minimum number of pages; bibliography does not follow MLA format	Report meets minimum number of pages; includes all items in checklist; follows MLA format	Report exceeds minimum requirements
Visuals	Visuals detract from report; do not add to understanding of guiding questions	Visuals add detail to the report; show evidence of design elements	Visuals add detail and greater depth of understanding; creative design elements enhance project

Even carefully worded praise can encourage students to self-evaluate: "What do you think is the best?" "What are you most proud of?" To help students see the relationship between effort and success, try "You really tried hard and it shows. Look at how many more you got right this time." "You stuck with it without giving up. Super!" "You can do it if you try."

Our goal is to give students a sense of control over their success or failure. Added to this, we must encourage them to persevere when setbacks occur. It's better for them to feel guilt when they didn't work hard enough than to feel shame because they don't think they have the ability. They'll give up if they attribute failure to lack of ability; they're more likely to persevere if they attribute failure to lack of effort. And, remember, only compare their performance to their past performances—not to other students.

✄ Figure 4.13
SKILLS LOG FOR YOUNG CHILDREN

Letting young children keep their own skills log allows them to track how their skills are growing. The teacher can use a developmental checklist of skills as a guide in developing a checklist for students.

I can do the following tasks:

1. Point to the front and back of a book.

2. Print these letters:

3. Name these letters:

4. Say these rhymes:

5. Write my name:

※   ※   ※

The skills provided in this chapter will help students both in the classroom and in the workplace. They are included in most lists of performance standards as applied learning (*New Standards,* 1997, p. 244). Empowered with the tools necessary for learning to take place, all students should succeed. In *Beyond Success,* Biro (1995, p. 107) paraphrases Coach John Wooden: "Success is peace of mind, which is a direct result of self-satisfaction in knowing you've done the best of which you are capable." If we can convince our reluctant learners that their effort will pay off in greater success and we model the belief that success is improvement, not perfection in our classrooms, then we, too, have achieved success.

5

Integrating Self-Management into the Curriculum

I t's not unusual to hear teachers ask "Where will I find the time to teach these self-management skills?" With the push for higher standards, more accountability, increased testing, and perform-ance-based assessment, there really is no excess time in the teaching schedule. There is a mad rush to get through the curriculum. The goal of this chapter is to provide examples of how to teach the many skills necessary for a successful classroom through the existing curriculum. These skills are not only essential for the classroom, they're crucial for success on the job, in family life, and with friends.

Our task is to align state standards to the goals of classroom management. These goals are to establish a community of learners who feel bonded and connected; who exhibit self-discipline, perseverance, and take responsibility for learning. A community of learners is not reached through admonishment or by giving cursory lip service: "I teach responsibility for 30 minutes every Friday." A community can only happen when, through practice, skills become habit. Habit is a way of acting, which is fixed through repetition.

A bad habit is also a way of acting fixed through repetition. It is well-established that children imitate what they see, so it should not be a surprise to see children use violence to problem solve when two-thirds of prime-time television shows include acts of violence. To both eliminate bad habits and provide for the needed repetition of good behaviors, we must immerse children with positive models. We can find models in all disciplines using positive exemplars that are aligned with state standards.

In this chapter, I'm using standards in the Language Arts and Social Studies to model the alignment process. The standards are from *Essential Academic Learning Requirements* (Washington State Commission on Student Learning, 1998) and the New Standards (National Center on Education and the Economy and the University of Pittsburgh, 1997). These are representative of the standards found in most states and districts.

A school should not be a preparation for life. A school should be life.

—ELBERT HUBBARD,
PUBLISHER, EDITOR,
AND WRITER

Reading Standards

When teaching reading, a teacher makes decisions about

- What the students will read
- What the students should know and be able to do with the reading
- What performances demonstrate that achievement

Many reading standards are skills based or content-free standards describing what the student should know and be able to do with what was read. When the selection of the standard has been made, the next step is to identify appropriate literary selections— what the students will read. The strategic selection of reading material can provide opportunity for the simultaneous teaching to standards and to self-management skills—thereby providing that needed repetition of good behaviors.

Select Your Standard

These are examples of standards that can be used for both academic and self-management goals.

- The student builds vocabulary through reading.
- The student analyzes, interprets, and synthesizes what is read.
- The student reads for the literary experience of understanding self and others.
- The student reads at least 25 books or book equivalents each year.
- The student reads and comprehends at least four book forms about one issue or subject, or four books by a single writer or in a single genre.
- The student reads and comprehends informational materials, making connections to related topics and relating new information to prior knowledge and experience.
- The student reads aloud in a way that makes meaning clear to listeners, with rhythm, flow, and meter that sound like everyday speech.

One way to counter moral illiteracy is to acquaint youngsters with stories and histories that can give them a common reference point and supply them with a stock of good examples.

—William Kilpatrick

Select Reading Materials

When selecting reading material, you can choose from a plethora of great literature that provides models of self-discipline, problem-solving, respect, and taking responsibility. The reading material selection is an opportunity to provide repeated exposure to what appropriate behaviors look like, how to recognize them in context, and how to transfer the behaviors to their own lives. When Bennett (1996) organized the anthology, *Book of Virtues*, he made the task of selecting relevant literature even easier. Literary selections are organized around themes such as perseverance, self-discipline, compassion, responsibility, and work ethic. In his anthologies for younger children, Bennett (1997) examines character traits through heroes. Self-control is modeled in the story of Jackie Robinson and the character trait of empathy is celebrated through a story about Mother Teresa.

From the rich selection of Native American tales and stories from the Brothers Grimm and *Aesop's Fables*, teachers can choose literature to inspire students. The lessons taught by fables with respect to right or wrong assist children with their own decision making. In his books of poetry, Silverstein (1981; 1996) adds humor to the study of human behavior with poems like "Screamin' Millie" (for anger management), "Headphone Harold" (for listening), and "Whatif" (for perseverance).

Ideally, as you develop a curriculum map for the year and make literature selections, group your titles around self-management themes. Figure 5.1 is a sample of a curriculum map for reading for the upper grades.

Plan Activities and Achievement

Literature selections can be used throughout a well-balanced reading program, which includes reading aloud to students, guided reading at students' instructional level, shared reading, and independent reading. Specific activities to integrate the literature selection with our goals might include

• Read aloud. Reading aloud a wisdom story daily provides a perfect format for a whole-class or small group discussion of the author's message, and an opportunity to relate the message to the students' own experiences. A 6th grade teacher reads one primary level "wisdom" book to her class every Monday. Students then share the wisdom from the author's message and write a quote on a Wisdom Chart. After reading Dr. Seuss's *Oh, the Places You'll Go!* (1990), quotes on the Wisdom Chart included "I am the conductor of my life." "I won't get to my destination without trying."

• Shared reading. Students may take a poem, short story, or

Life is a story. And because stories communicate life's realities, they play an important role in studying and understanding all dimensions of the human experience.

—J. Lea Smith and Holly Johnson

✄ Figure 5.1
LITERATURE SELECTIONS

Use the following literature selections to help align curriculum with standards and themes of behavior.

. . . .

Thoughtfulness, Self-Awareness
Armstrong, W. (1969). *Sounder*. New York: Harper & Row.
Bennett, W. (1995). *The Moral Compass: Stories for a Life's Journey* (Chapter 7, What We Live By). New York: Simon & Schuster.
Paterson, K. (1990). *Jacob Have I Loved*. Santa Barbara, CA: Cornerstone Books.

. . . .

Perseverance, Effort, Confidence, Industriousness
Bennett, W. (1995). *The Moral Compass: Stories for a Life's Journey* (Chapter 3, Standing Fast). New York: Simon & Schuster.
Cleary, B. (1991). *Strider*. New York: Morrow Junior Books.
O'Dell, S. (1987). *Island of the Blue Dolphins*. Santa Barbara: ABC-Clio.
Sperry, A. (1990). *Call It Courage*. New York: Aladdin Books.
Taylor, M. (1989). *Roll of Thunder, Hear My Cry*. Santa Barbara, CA: Cornerston Publishers.

. . . .

Responsibility, Initiative, Problem Solving
Bauer, M. (1989). *On My Honor*. Boston: G. K. Hall.
Bennett, W. (1993). *The Book of Virtues: A Treasury of Great Moral Stories* (Chapter 3, Responsibility). New York: Simon & Schuster.
Lowry, L. (1989). *Number the Stars*. Boston: Houghton Mifflin Co.

. . . .

Problem Solving, Self-Discipline, Impulse Control
Bennett, W. (1993). *The Book of Virtues: A Treasury of Great Moral Stories*. (Chapter 1, Self Discipline). New York: Simon & Schuster.
Lowry, L. (1994). *The Giver*.
Stevenson, R. (1883). *Treasure Island*.

. . . .

Caring, Thoughtfulness
Bennett, W. (1995). *The Moral Compass: Stories for a Life's Journey* (Chapter 4, Easing the Path). New York: Simon & Schuster.
Campbell, B. (1986). *Taking Care of Yoki*. 1st Harper Trophy ed.
Creech, S. (1994). *Walk Two Moons*. New York: HarperCollins.
MacLachlan, P. (1985). *Sara, Plain and Tall*. Santa Barbara, CA: ABC-Clio.
Speare, E. (1983). *The Sign of the Beaver*. Santa Barbara, CA: ABC-Clio.

. . . .

Teamwork, Cooperative Skills
Bennett, W. (1993). *The Book of Virtues: A Treasury of Great Moral Stories* (Chapter 4, Friendship). New York: Simon & Schuster.

⚹ Figure 5.2
WORD BANK FOR EMOTIONS

Students can use word banks to build vocabulary and to improve reading comprehension. In this case, the word bank is designed to help students explore the idea of emotions and feelings in a particular novel. The teacher has supplied some words and the students are expected to add more words and insert the page numbers that indicate when a character is feeling that emotion.

exasperate p. _____	aloof p. _____	temerity p. _____
contempt p. _____	disdain p. _____	placid p. _____
pride p. _____	imperious p. _____	

famous speech and practice it for reading aloud, using a reader's theater format as they passionately portray the selection, making the meaning coming alive for the listeners.

• Guided reading. A guided reading lesson might introduce the story elements of problem and solution, a perfect vehicle to analyze perseverance and problem solving.

• Independent reading. Choosing a single subject, such as self-discipline, the teacher may gather a variety of reading materials (poetry, novels, short stories, biographies) for independent reading.

In addition to planning activities for a balanced reading program, you must plan for student performances that demonstrate achievement of the standard. For example, in developing the standard "to build vocabulary through reading" here are some appropriate activities:

• Students can develop an ABC Book of Feelings to extend vocabulary and comprehension of their reading (A—angry, amused; B—belligerent, bemused).

• Students can develop a Word Bank for emotions and feelings as they read (see Figure 5.2).

To measure student understanding of literary elements, provide graphic organizers to assist students with the analysis. The organizers in figures 5.3, 5.4, 5.5, and 5.6 were developed to help students understand character traits.

✂ **Figure 5.3**
CHARACTER QUALITY CHART

Ask students to use a chart to identify the qualities they admire in a character found in a book, play, or short story. Exploring the qualities of a character can lead to expanding awareness about personal qualities.

Character's Name	Quality and Example (List quality and give specific example)	Chapter or pages

�* Figure 5.4
CHARACTER COMPARISON

Ask each student to pick a character in a book and to fill out the chart by comparing the personality of the character with the student's own personality.

YOU

CHARACTER
IN

How are you alike?

How are you different with regard to

PATIENCE

RESOURCEFULNESS

SELF-AWARENESS

Figure 5.5
CHOOSE A FRIEND

To extend students' thoughts about the books they read and self-awareness
of desirable character traits, use this activity to help them pick a character from
the book as a friend. To help adjust the level of the activity for upper-grade
students, have them write a paper about their choice.

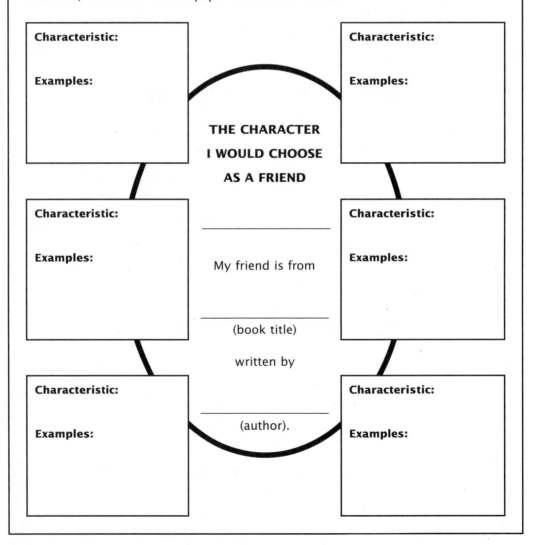

Characteristic:

Examples:

Characteristic:

Examples:

THE CHARACTER
I WOULD CHOOSE
AS A FRIEND

Characteristic:

Examples:

Characteristic:

Examples:

_____
My friend is from

_____
(book title)

written by

Characteristic:

Examples:

_____
(author).

Characteristic:

Examples:

✁ Figure 5.6
CHARACTER COMPARISON

To measure student understanding of literary elements, such as character, give them graphic organizers. For example, ask students to fill in character names and to provide specific details from text for each social skill. As they work on the organizer, it can help them build an awareness of their own social interactions.

Book title: _____

Author: _____

I think the character with the best overall social skills is

_____.

```
                        ┌──────────────────────┐
                        │    SOCIAL SKILLS     │
                        └──────────────────────┘
                                   │
        ┌──────────────┬───────────┴───────────┬──────────────┐
   ┌─────────┐    ┌─────────┐         ┌─────────┐    ┌─────────┐
   │Listening│    │ Sharing │         │ Manners │    │ Empathy │
   └─────────┘    └─────────┘         └─────────┘    └─────────┘
        │              │                   │              │
   ┌─────────┐    ┌─────────┐         ┌─────────┐    ┌─────────┐
   │         │    │         │         │         │    │         │
   └─────────┘    └─────────┘         └─────────┘    └─────────┘
        │              │                   │              │
   ┌─────────┐    ┌─────────┐         ┌─────────┐    ┌─────────┐
   │         │    │         │         │         │    │         │
   └─────────┘    └─────────┘         └─────────┘    └─────────┘
        │              │                   │              │
   ┌─────────┐    ┌─────────┐         ┌─────────┐    ┌─────────┐
   │         │    │         │         │         │    │         │
   └─────────┘    └─────────┘         └─────────┘    └─────────┘
```

Writing Standards

Writing provides opportunities for students to express their thoughts and feelings about social and personal issues related to classroom behaviors. Writing also provides the vehicle for students to demonstrate the knowledge and skills gained in the other disciplines (e.g., a response to literature). Figure 5.7 is an example of how to select writing standards and how to align them with goals of classroom management.

Viewing and Speaking Standards

In this section, we'll focus only on viewing and speaking standards. The one standard that appears in almost every list of communication standards:

The student uses communication strategies and skills to work effectively with others

- Works cooperatively as a member of a group
- Uses language to interact effectively and responsibly with others

The standard, using communication strategies and skills to work effectively with others, is in itself a goal of classroom management. It gives the teacher permission to take time to teach the enabling skills. Repeated practice with this standard would be impossible without the use of small, cooperative groups in the classroom. Benchmarks or enabling skills for this standard include giving compliments, encouragement, expressing feelings, and demonstrating respect. For example, practice can be provided for giving compliments:

- When students give their oral reports in class, listeners may fill out feedback forms for the speaker, complimenting them on the best parts of the report.

We would be wasting a great opportunity if we failed to use our curriculum as a vehicle for developing values and ethical awareness.

—T<small>HOMAS</small> L<small>ICKONA</small>

✗ Figure 5.7
WRITING STANDARDS ALIGNED WITH GOALS
OF CLASSROOM MANAGEMENT

Here's an example of how to select writing standards and merge them with the goals of classroom management strategies.

Writing Standards	Classroom Management Activity
The student writes clearly and effectively.	Analysis of the significance of a quotation or proverb develops critical thinking skills as well as character (e.g., "No act of kindness, no matter how small, is ever wasted."—Aesop).
The student writes in a variety of forms (e.g., journals, poems, and essays) for different audiences and purposes (e.g., telling stories and persuading).	Writing from the character's point of view is a building block for empathy. Students keep a diary, writing in the first person, reflecting upon the character's feelings about life events. As students learn how to read another's feelings, classroom community is enhanced.
The student produces a report that develops a controlling idea that conveys a perspective on the subject.	To focus students on classroom issues, assign topics such as "Is violence ever justified?" or "Is success perfection or improvement?"
The student produces a response to literature that produces a judgment that is interpretive, analytic, evaluative, or reflective.	After analyzing the characters in a novel, students select the character who exhibits the highest emotional intelligence and support their selection with evidence of high emotional intelligence. Or, students can compare the conflict and resolution cycle in a novel to events in real life. *(continued)*

✎ **Figure 5.7** (continued)
WRITING STANDARDS ALIGNED WITH GOALS OF CLASSROOM MANAGEMENT

Writing Standards	Classroom Management Activity
The student produces a narrative account (fictional or autobiographical) that establishes a situation, plot, point of view, setting, and conflict.	Write their own fable, selecting the animal character, the setting and the moral. Examples include • Friends are made by many acts and lost by only one. • One learns manners from those who have none. Or, student may write about their journey through life and reflect upon their own skills in resolving conflicts.
The student writes for different audiences and purposes, including persuading others.	To develop community and encourage caring, students identify issues that concern them. A class meeting provides the venue, a persuasive essay the mechanism (e.g., an editorial in a school newspaper about hallway safety).

• Give students sticky notes to write compliments and place on other students' work that is displayed in the classroom.

Some reminders for setting up cooperative learning in the classroom are (Cummings, 1990):

1. Learning how to work in a small group is "a process, not an event."

2. Keep group size small (2–5).

3. Select group members carefully. (The proactive teacher does not place all students with poor social skills in one group.)

4. Remember the stages of group development

    a. FORMING: host an ice breaker or getting to know you activity

    b. STORMING: minimize stress by assigning roles (e.g., recorder, or sheriff; or use team structures such as numbered heads or round robin)

    c. NORMING: set up norms of behavior (how to express feelings, how to disagree in an appropriate way); teach and practice these one at a time

5. Provide specific feedback to the teams on their group skills. This can include praise from the teacher, having a team member record group interactions, reporting to the larger group, or self-evaluation.

Viewing Habits

A relatively new standard in most state documents relates to the analysis of mass communication and its impact on emotions and behavior:

The student makes informed judgments about television, radio, and film productions; evaluates the role of the media in focusing attention and in forming an opinion.

To make students more aware of the effects of the media on their lives, including classroom atmosphere, have them analyze their viewing habits. In the *New Standards* (1997, page 49) a Media Viewing Log asks students to record

- Time spent
- Program viewed
- Other activities done while viewing
- Activities not done in favor of viewing
- Benefits of viewing
- Detriments of viewing

When right standards are consistently presented, the motion picture exercises the most powerful influences. It builds character, develops right ideals, inoculates correct principles. . . .
—THE MOTION PICTURE CODE, 1930–1966

After keeping a log for a week, students then evaluate the role of the media in their lives.

In *Screen Smarts* (1996), DeGaetano and Bander provide parents and teachers more than 100 activities to develop critical thinking about television viewing. Even very young children can tally the number of acts of violence they see in a single program, count the number of compliments, or chart the number of put-downs and inappropriate name-calling occurrences.

Social Studies Standards

Learn from others what to pursue and what to avoid, and let your teachers be the lives of others.

—*DIONYSIUS CATA (4TH CENTURY, A.D.)*

Whether you select content-free standards or content-specific standards (e.g., Washington State History; U.S. government), there is often a natural fit with the goals of classroom management. The study of history alone should include more than names and dates; it should include the compelling moral and social issues of the time. The standards in Figure 5.8 have natural connections to our goals.

To better understand the interrelationships between major events, their outcomes, and social-emotional skills, fill in a grid similar to Figure 5.9. Take each issue and give concrete examples of how these skills played a key role in the outcome.

To teach the standards related to government and citizenship, use *Judicious Discipline* (Gathercoal, 1990) to provide concrete examples for connecting the U.S. democratic system, particularly the Bill of Rights, to the classroom. Students should see that the classroom community is modeled after the democratic society in which we live. What may be confusing for students, though, is how a school can have rules that infringe upon their rights as an individual (e.g., freedom of speech, the right to bear arms). The book shows how to teach the concept of compelling state interest (. . . in some cases the needs and interests of the majority weigh greater than those of an individual). This legal principle gives teachers the ". . . professional

Figure 5.8
ALIGNING SOCIAL STUDIES STANDARDS WITH CLASSROOM MANAGEMENT

There is often a natural fit between learning standards and the goals of classroom management. For example, the study of history includes names, dates, and the compelling moral and social issues of the time.

Standards	**Prompts aligned with classroom management**
The student understands the impact of ideas on history and social change. ▪ Investigates the cause and effect relationships of historical events ▪ Examines major issues, people, and events with emphasis on change and continuity, growth and conflict (e.g., the civil rights movement) ▪ Examines how cultural elements impact society ▪ Examines how ideas conflict with each other, impact our lives (e.g., free speech, communism versus democracy, individual freedom versus the common good)	▪ Why is self-control important in international politics? ▪ How are decisions made at a national level similar or dissimilar to decisions made in our classroom? ▪ Are there two sides to every conflict? Give an example from history and one from our classroom. ▪ When have conflicts been solved without resorting to violence? Provide examples from a national level and from a school level. ▪ When violence has been used to settle conflicts, both in and out of school—what has been achieved? ▪ What are the skills a diplomat needs? How would these skills be useful in the classroom?
The student understands the rights and responsibilities of citizenship: ▪ How rights and responsibilities relate to classroom rules, family obligations, freedom of the press	▪ Develop a Rights and Responsibilities chart for your classroom. – "I have the right to be listened to, therefore, I have the responsibility to listen to others."

(continued)

✂ **Figure 5.8** *(continued)*
**ALIGNING SOCIAL STUDIES STANDARDS
WITH CLASSROOM MANAGEMENT**

Standards	Prompts aligned with classroom management
• Explain democracy as a balance between your own rights and the rights of others (playground rules, common courtesy, sharing)	– "I have the right not to be made fun of, therefore, I have the responsibility not to make fun of others."
The student understands the principles of the U.S. democracy *(included in the Declaration of Independence and the Constitution):* • Explains ideals such as individual human dignity, justice, equality • Understands how citizens influence government to solve problems (through community service, voting, lobbying)	• Write a biography of one person from the last century who has influenced the development of the democratic ideals of human dignity, justice, and equality. Share the biography at a biography fair. • Students identify school issues that concern them and write a persuasive letter to the school newspaper or a political representative about a school issue (e.g., hall safety or the need for a crosswalk).

---

responsibility to prohibit student behaviors when the exercise of those rights seriously affects the welfare of the school." (p. 19)

The Hero as a Guide

Do you ever wonder if we are lacking modern heroes on which to pattern our behavior? Frankly, some athletes, musicians, and movie stars are not appropriate role models for our youth.

Nevertheless, it is through the study of human behavior that we can best understand ourselves. As students study how the charac-

✂ Figure 5.9
RELATING SOCIAL-EMOTIONAL SKILLS TO HISTORICAL EVENTS

Use a table to help your students become aware of the role that social-emotional skills play in our world.

Events	Self-Discipline	Social Skills	Empathy
1770s • Boston Tea Party • First and Second Continental Congresses • Declaration of Independence			
1780s • Articles of Confederation • Northwest Ordinance • Washington—First President • French Revolution			
1790s • Bill of Rights • Adams—President • Alien and Sedition Acts			

teristics of an individual can influence history, let them pick a hero and analyze the character traits responsible for the hero's success (see Figure 5.10).

The final exam I give for a course on emotional intelligence asks teachers (or their students) to write an article for an imaginary new journal, *Emotional Intelligence.* They are to select a person of the decade (or century) who reflects the components of emotional intelligence and has most influenced history—positively or negatively. This assignment is aligned with the social studies standards

• Understanding of how personal characteristics of people influence history
• Students demonstrating effective communication skills and decision making skills

Students are to use a rubric to evaluate emotional intelligence. The basic scale is 1 = not observable, inappropriate, skills poorly applied; 2 = developing, skills applied inconsistently; 3 = consistently exhibits skills. For a more complete rubric, see Figure 5.11.

There has been amazing consistency in the selection of candidates for this award from the hundreds of exams I have scored. Nominees have included Steven Spielberg, Michael Jordan, Jimmy Carter, Mother Teresa, Oprah, Bill Clinton, Saddam Hussein, and Princess Diana. Teachers and students who have used the rubric have had similar revelations. Nominees they felt would be the winner did not pass scrutiny in all categories. One political figure scored high in all categories but empathy; in addition he had inconsistent ratings for social skills. His polished social skills were used to further his own interests at the expense of others. "Charm and social polish in themselves do not add up to competence at influence; social skill in the service of oneself, and to the detriment of the group as a whole, is sooner or later recognized as a charade"

We need education in the obvious more than investigation of the obscure.

—OLIVER WENDELL HOLMES, JR.

✄ Figure 5.10
EXAMINING THE CHARACTERISTICS OF A HERO

As students study how the characteristics of an individual can influence history, let them pick a hero and analyze the character traits responsible for the hero's success. Ask them to use this chart to think about their hero.

MY HERO IS:

Heroic Traits	Why is this person my hero? Here are examples to support each of the heroic characteristics.
Endurance	
Sacrifice	
Courage	
Compassion	

✄ Figure 5.11
RUBRIC TO EVALUATE EMOTIONAL INTELLIGENCE

Let your students use this rubric to evaluate a hero and to become aware of what emotional intelligence means. Later in the year they can use the rubric to evaluate their own emotional intelligence.

SCALE AREA	1 Not observable; inappropriate; skills poorly applied	2 Developing; skills applied inconsistently	3 Consistently exhibits skills
Self-Awareness	Lets emotions guide behaviors (e.g., anger, fear, irritation); does not learn from experiences		Knows personal strengths and limitations; knows own emotional state and its effects; self-confident; intuitive
Self-Regulation	Lacks self-control; impulsive; aggressive (perhaps a bully); does not delay gratification; is dishonest and undependable		Manages moods; controls impulses; takes responsibility; exhibits self-control
Self-Motivated	Does not finish assignments; sense of depression; feels hopeless; gives up easily; does not set realistic goals or work toward goal completion		Sets reasonable goals and measures accomplishment; persistent in spite of setbacks; sense of optimism and hope

✂ **Figure 5.11** *(continued)*
RUBRIC TO EVALUATE EMOTIONAL INTELLIGENCE

SCALE AREA	1 Not observable; inappropriate; skills poorly applied	2 Developing; skills applied inconsistently	3 Consistently exhibits skills
Empathy	Is not sensitive to others' feelings; unable to take another's perspective; not interested in helping others; feels no guilt or remorse		Recognizes emotional state of others and responds appropriately; acts on others' needs and concerns
Social Skills	Not a team player; avoids social contacts; does not collaborate and share in a group; difficult time making friends		Participates well in groups; good communication skills; listens attentively; builds respectful working relationships

(Goleman, 1998, p. 174). The surprise for many students were nominees that they'd picked to have an evil or negative influence on the world ranked high in self-awareness and self-motivation.

The response from both teachers and students who have completed this exercise has been positive. One middle school student wrote, "I thought this would be a boring assignment. It turned out to be the most exciting thing we've done this year."

An extension of this exercise is to ask students to use the rubric for self-evaluation or to evaluate characters in novels.

The Thematic, Integrated Unit

The thematic, integrated unit is a unit designed to study the interrelationships between the disciplines. While this unit has been popular in the elementary grades, it has become increasingly common at the secondary level as more teachers are teaming and using block scheduling. It is perhaps even easier to integrate the goals of classroom management into this broader unit, beginning with the careful selection of a theme and guiding questions. Many of the themes recommended for units align with the concepts taught in classroom management—community, connections, conflict and change, power, systems, perceptions, relationships, and beliefs.

Guiding questions are the big ideas that cut across the disciplines and deepen understanding of major concepts. The guiding questions below can be linked to better understanding the goals of classroom management, as well as a deeper understanding of the disciplines including social studies and science.

To take these guiding questions to the next step, look at the connections between the skills stressed in this book with the questions in Figure 5.12.

The remaining steps for completing an integrated unit are similar to those we just reviewed for matching standards and activities. For the integrated unit you need decide how many disciplines and related standards align with the theme, taking care not to force a fit.

Report Cards

Moving beyond state and district standards, examine your district report cards. Most have categories reflective of the goals of class-

Education has for its object the formation of character.

—Herbert Spencer (1851)

✄ Figure 5.12
ALIGNING GUIDING QUESTIONS WITH CLASSROOM MANAGEMENT

Guiding questions are the big ideas that cut across the disciplines and deepen understanding of major concepts. The guiding questions below—on the idea of change—can be linked to better understanding the goals of classroom management, as well as to a deeper understanding of the disciplines, including social studies and science.

Guiding Questions for Change	Skills
<ul><li>Can change be good or bad?</li><li>Is change inevitable?</li><li>Is change necessary for growth?</li></ul>	<ul><li>Self-control and impulse control</li><li>Persistence and perseverance</li><li>Recognizing problems</li><li>Goal setting</li><li>Decision making</li><li>Taking responsibility</li><li>Cooperation with others who are working hard to get smart</li></ul>
Guiding Questions for Relationships	**Skills**
<ul><li>How do I relate to my family?</li><li>How do I relate to my school?</li><li>How do I relate to my neighborhood?</li><li>What are cause-and-effect relationships?</li><li>Do I have control over cause-and-effect relationships?</li></ul>	<ul><li>Perspective taking</li><li>Respect</li><li>Listening</li><li>Awareness of feelings</li><li>Making friends</li></ul>

**Figure 5.13
REPORT CARD**

The ideal report card has a place for both the teacher and the student to rate the student's behavior. Use this sample to open the conversation with your students.

	Student	Teacher
I express my emotions appropriately.		
I use anger control strategies.		
I am able to resist impulsive behavior.		
I have a positive attitude.		
I plan carefully.		
I use my time wisely and produce high-quality work.		
I see setbacks as temporary.		
I willingly accept responsibility for my actions.		
I show concern for the feelings of others.		
I am helpful to others.		
I get along with my classmates.		
I contribute and do my share of group work.		
I work well independently.		

room management, such as "to teach students the social, study, and work skills necessary to establish a community of learners." In the progress report, teachers are asked to evaluate students on behaviors including

- Follows classroom, playground, and school rules
- Follows both written and oral directions
- Uses appropriate language
- Takes responsibility for own behaviors
- Respects others
- Brings appropriate materials to class

- Keeps working space (desk or table) organized
- Completes work on time
- Stays on task
- Works independently
- Work is neat and legible

In addition to the above skills, students are graded on subjects, including reading, handwriting, math, language, music, and science. Imagine a student receiving a failing grade in reading if reading had not been explicitly taught in class. Likewise, how can you evaluate a student as "needs improvement" in the category "respects others" if the same time and energy wasn't spent teaching respect.

Instead of discrete categories to evaluate behavior, most secondary report cards provide space for teacher comments. The list of suggested grade comments parallels those categories found on elementary report cards:

- You demonstrate attentive listening skills. (Or, You need to limit socializing; You need to pay more attention during instruction.)
- You come to class prepared to work. (Or, You don't come prepared to work.)
- You have worked well in groups. (Or, You need to work at improving relationships with others, your inappropriate behavior distracts your progress.)
- You demonstrate good motivation and effort. (Or, You need to develop better self control; You need to improve your study habits.)

Of course, the ideal report card might have a category for both teacher and student reflection. See Figure 5.13 for a sample. The challenge for the teacher is to show where the enabling skills for these categories have been explicitly taught and practiced before a summative assessment is given.

❧   ❧   ❧

Tom Landry, former Dallas football coach, reminds us that "setting a goal is not the main thing. It is deciding how you to go about achieving it and staying with that plan." The worthy goal of building a community of learners who feel bonded and connected; who exhibit self-discipline, perseverance, and take responsibility for learning can be achieved in alliance with district standards. It takes deliberate and careful planning, but it can be done.

Preventing Misbehavior

I have made a ceaseless effort not to ridicule, not to bewail,
not to scorn human actions, but to understand.

—BARUCH SPINOZA

A frequent complaint about Health Maintenance Organizations (HMOs) is that they shove medication at the patient to treat the symptoms while ignoring the cause. We have to be careful that we are not doing the same thing in education. If the symptom is misbehavior, we don't want to be guilty of stopping it with punishment and ignoring the cause. Sylwester (2000) puts a different spin on this philosophy:

> In sum, the classroom management literature tends to view management as a teacher responsibility and misbehavior as a problem that teachers have with students rather than the reverse. Regrettably, teacher misbehavior may well be the cause of some (if not much) disruptive student misbehavior. (pp.1–2)

What Is Misbehavior?

Your class will misbehave. That's a given. Misbehavior may range from small, annoying disturbances to those that are life-threatening. When teachers are asked to list classroom misbehavior, the list includes:

- Playing with a ruler or pencil or other objects[1]
- Tapping[1]
- Whistling or making inappropriate sounds[1]
- Saying "shut up"[1]
- Ignoring or not listening to the teacher or other students[1]
- Leaning back in chairs (two legs off the floor)
- Passing notes
- Invading the personal space of others (physically picking on or intimidating others)[1]
- Tattling
- Teasing or delivering put-downs
- Not sharing and taking materials that belong to someone else[1]
- Performing self-abuse
- Making noise or inappropriately using manipulatives[1]
- Eating or chewing gum
- Sleeping in class or daydreaming[1]
- Talking during instruction[1]
- Complaining, whining, and pouting
- Spitting
- Being off task (e.g., talking when they're supposed to be singing)[1]
- Telling lies
- Writing on or destroying other people's property
- Putting on make-up or lotion, brushing hair
- Blurting out answers[1]
- Asking inappropriate and insincere questions
- Arguing with the teacher, talking back, refusing to do work (won't take "no" for an answer)[1]
- Swearing, using inappropriate language
- Doing work from another class
- Cheating or copying
- Reading magazines, books, using headphones during instruction[1]

- Flipping off another student or the teacher; insulting others
- Acting out or behaving in a manner that suggests sexual harassment
  - Showing or stating open defiance (e.g., "make me")
  - Throwing desk, books, or objects at students or teacher[1]
  - Making threats
  - Screaming, yelling, tantrums[1]
  - Hitting others[1]
  - Using weapons

There's always quite a list of misbehaviors. And the list of intervention for misbehaviors is just as extensive. Rather than focusing on the interventions, however, we'll focus on the cause of the misbehavior and what we can do to prevent it.

The Presence of Threat

Some classroom experiences may provoke strong emotion from some students and interfere with their learning. Many of the misbehaviors from the list are the result of strong emotion. Students cannot learn with the presence of threat or excessive worry. In fact, stress causes the release of certain hormones that hamper memory. Think about the time you walked into a classroom after preparing for the test and your mind became a blank. In the classroom, threatening events may be physical, emotional, or intellectual. Fortunately, it's possible to minimize or eliminate many of these threats.

Intellectual Threats

Some students may feel danger or harm from intellectual threats, real or imagined. For some students, simply the possibility

---

[1] *These misbehaviors are also characteristic of ADD/ADHD children.*

of one of the following actions gives them feeling of impending danger or harm:

- Having to work in a group
- Hearing an announcement of a pop quiz
- Receiving unclear directions
- Being called upon to answer in front of the class
- Fearing failure in a particular subject
- Being unable to hear a lesson because of noise from other students
- Posting of grades or having them read aloud in class
- Being afraid of name calling such as stupid or dumb or seeing disgusted reactions from peers
- Feeling intellectually inferior
- Feeling unable to complete the assignment on time
- Being afraid of reading aloud in class

Intellectual threats are easier to control than physical or emotional threats. The above stressors may be minimized or eliminated by using the following strategies:

- Provide students a choice of working alone or with a group to alleviate the fear of small group work.
- Minimize test anxiety by announcing when the test will be and the type of test to expect. If possible, provide sample test items (e.g., list 10 essay questions and explain that the test will include four questions from the list). This strategy can be used with all kids, K–12.
- Reduce the number of test items on a single page and double space the questions.
- Let students know the grade is based on the content of the answers, not mechanics, spelling, or penmanship.
- Provide an option of taking the test orally or audiotaping answers.

• Put directions of three steps or more in writing. List the steps (not in paragraph form) and number them. Ask students to repeat the directions. Have students use a highlighter pen to note key points.

• Provide printed copies of directions instead of having students copy directions from the board or take notes on verbal directions.

• Use cooperative learning structures to provide students opportunities to discuss an answer with their peers. If their number is called, they may preface their answer with "My team says the answer is . . ."

• Students who know what their grades are on a daily basis are less likely to experience the anxiety of how they're doing in a class. In the upper grades, provide time for students to record the grades on all classwork that is graded and returned. Check assignments sheets on a regular basis to be sure they are kept up-to-date.

• Give lectures and directions only when students exhibit listening behavior. If this is one of those days when it seems impossible to reach calm, then abandon ship! Shift to small group or independent work.

• A student doesn't have to be called dumb or stupid to feel stupid—which may be the result of posting or calling grades out in front of the class. The solution to this threat is to eliminate the practice. Students should be competing against themselves (their previous scores)—not other students and their scores.

• During the first few weeks of school, set up norms for behavior such as no insults. A banner across the front of the room "You have just entered an insult-free zone" serves as a constant visual reminder of norms.

Often the intellectual threat expresses itself in frustration. We hear it as whining or back talk:

- This is dumb.
- Why do we have to do this?
- This is way too much work.
- I'll never be able to do it.
- How am I supposed to know this stuff?
- Do I have to do it?

Take a big, deep breath and show your willingness to listen and assist. Look beyond the complaints to diagnose and treat the cause:

- Let's go over the directions again and try to make sense out of them together.
- Let's begin it together until you get comfortable with the assignment.
- Why don't you show me how you tried the first problem so I find out the steps you already know.

Think of how many tricks students use to avoid answering questions in class or beginning an assignment. If students fail, they'll look stupid in front of their peers, therefore they'd rather fake an illness or have an urgent need to go to the bathroom. We must learn to recognize the disguises students use—often misbehavior—for fear of failure.

Emotional Threats

Emotional threats may overlap intellectual threats and vary dramatically among students. Emotional threats include

- Negative language, bullying, intimidation and other forms of put-downs
- Fear of being disciplined by an adult in front of peers
- Boyfriend and girlfriend troubles
- Coping with divorce or other family trauma
- Fear of an overbearing family, family reaction to poor grades

- Fear of looking different, not having the right clothes; not fitting in
  - Unrealistic goals (I want to be a professional athlete)
  - Fear of being a nerd
  - Difficulty making friends

Emotional threats reach a peak in adolescence and present quite a challenge to the teacher. The other chapters in this book have stressed the need to create an emotionally safe environment for students so that learning can occur. The sections in this chapter related to childhood depression and anger provide additional ideas on minimizing emotional threats. The vigilance of the teacher is needed to refer some students for grief counseling, anger management, and other forms of support. With today's troubled youth, a team approach is needed.

Physical Threats

With the number of school tragedies apparently on the rise, it's not surprising that students feel physically threatened. Physical threats include

- Fear of pushing, shoving, tripping in the hall
- Fear of having personal items stolen
- Worries about plans to escalate a disagreement after school
- Verbal threats about impending violence
- Fear of being caught up in a fight
- Fear of weapons being used in school
- Being tired or not feeling well

The reality of these fears has increased in the past few years. A recent student found more than 50 percent of children ages 9–17 worried about dying young. And, 31 percent of children ages 12–17 know someone their age who carries a gun (Cohen, 1999). One tactic to minimize physical threats in the schools is to teach anger management. We also know that some major events—divorce, death, moving, birth of a sibling—cause such hurt and stress that the child tries to hurt back. These are the times to seek additional help for children.

In addition to becoming aware of the threats students feel today, we must become better at diagnosing body language and actions that betray students' feelings and finding ways to reduce the threat. Read the body language of students, then decide what to do differently. Are they afraid? Bored? Apathetic? Confused? Frustrated? Distressed? Irritated? Sullen? What nonverbal signals are they sending you? Are they slumping in chair, clenching their fists, staring into space, or sleeping? Sometimes the simple fix is a change of activity: "Stand up and explain this concept to the person behind you."

Nothing in life is to be feared. It is only to be understood.

—Marie Curie

Challenges from Today's Classroom Population

To better understand the misbehaviors in our classroom, let's look at what is behind the behaviors. If we understand the child, then we are equipped to make appropriate decisions. For example, with inclusion we have significantly more special needs students in the classroom. When the needs of the special needs children, or those of any children, aren't met—when students feel excluded—the consequence is misbehavior. In addition, students of the mass-media generation often exhibit the same behaviors used to describe Attention Deficit Disorder (ADD). It's more productive to change the environment to prevent inattentive and disruptive behaviors than to await their occurrence and react to them.

Increased anger is also a product of a mass media generation. According to Goleman (1995), anger is the most difficult emotion to control. Unless we give student strategies to manage their anger and for handling bullies, we will see increased aggression and turbulence in the classroom.

With the dramatic increase in childhood depression, Goleman (1995) argues that this epidemic should be prevented—not just treated. Prevention strategies, such as how to make friends and optimistic thinking, can be helpful in preventing self-destructive, antisocial, and other problem behaviors.

Although the prevention of misbehavior is the goal, you can be certain there will be times when intervention is necessary. Using the ideas in this chapter will help you concentrate on solutions rather than punishment.

Inclusion

With the practice of inclusion, many teachers have observed an increase in misbehavior in the classroom. Instead of jumping to the consequences of misbehavior, analyze the *W*s first:

Who: Who was involved? Was it a special-needs child? Do you have any ADD/ADHD children in your room? Do you have children with symptoms of depression? Any learning disabled students?

What: What happened? Was it major? Minor?

When: When did it happen? Was it during a transition? Independent work? Teacher talk? Small group work?

Where: Where did it happen?

Why: Why did it happen? Was it volitional?

How: How can you minimize the likelihood of it happening again?

Imagine having a visually impaired student in your classroom. If that student should walk into the classroom, bump into a table of supplies knocking them onto the floor, your first thought would be to move the table so it didn't happen again. You'd look at the cause, and not the behavior. It would never occur to you to punish the student for bumping into the table—you know he could not see it.

If only the disabilities of our included children were as obvious as those of the visually handicapped. In this section we look at what you can do *with* the student (not *to* the student) to prevent further misbehavior from occurring. First, let's look at the characteristics of some of our students.

Attention Deficit Disorder (ADD) and Attention Deficit Hyperactive Disorder (ADHD). Finding 99 ways to sit in a chair shows creativity and flexibility. However, when it disrupts the learning of others in the classroom or could be a potential safety issue, it becomes a management problem. When a child is trying to hug or hold hands or touch and the other child doesn't want to be involved, you may have a management problem. If you look back to the general list of misbehaviors in a classroom (pp. 116–117), those marked with a footnote are characteristic of ADD/ADHD children. How many of these students are in your classroom? The estimates range anywhere from 2 percent to 9.5 percent—that's one or two or even three students per class (Barkley, 1998).

Characteristics of Students from a Mass-Media Generation. Many students do not have the clinical diagnosis of ADD/ADHD, yet exhibit many of the behavioral symptoms. Healy (1998; 1994) has uncovered evidence showing that kid's brains really have changed. Today's children have brains that have been exposed to a flickering electronic field during their formative years instead of three-dimensional experiences necessary for normal wiring. "Their learning habits have been shaped by fast-paced media that reduce attention, listening, and problem-solving skills as they habituate the brain to rapid-fire visual input" (p. 40). Most 5-year-olds have watched between 4,000 and 5,000 hours of TV by the time they reach 1st grade—the equivalent of four years of college. That's valuable time wasted—time that should be spent exploring an enriched environment—developing the brain's social systems. "Television may be the single greatest deterrent to developing social and emotional skills."

(Shapiro, 1997, p. 35) Misbehavior is a natural product of a brain whose social-emotional wiring has been impaired.

Neuroimaging studies have shown prefrontal cortex problems that cause many of the misbehaviors noted above. Amen (1998, p. 132) found that prefrontal cortex dysfunction creates the following behaviors:

- Short attention span—frequently off-task
- Not listening, interrupting
- Impulsivity and lack of forethought
- Self-stimulation—restlessness, humming
- Seeking conflict
- Disorganization of time and personal space
- Moody, irritable, negative thinking
- Lethargy, apathy, lack of motivation
- Difficulty with expressing feelings or showing empathy

Changing the Environment. How do we deal with today's classroom? We need to change our approach, not the child. Change the environment because some of today's students cannot fit the traditional classroom. That is, placing an ADD/ADHD child in a classroom environment that doesn't allow students out of their seats without permission, doesn't allow talking without being called upon, and expects students to follow directions the first time they are given, sets an ADD/ADHD child up for failure. When the ADD/ADHD child doesn't comply with these demands, he's broken the class rules and is often given the negative consequences. As a result, too high a proportion of these children fail or become under-achievers. Frankly, the modifications that help special-needs children create a better learning community for all children.

To complain that these students should be on Ritalin or some other related drug to treat the neurochemical imbalance won't improve the behavior in classrooms. A drug cannot replace the creative teaching needed to help these students develop coping skills. These kids do not misbehave on purpose; instead, they may be desperately trying to be good. They need coping skills such as anger management techniques, goal setting skills, organizational strategies, how to delay gratification, and how to get rid of negative thinking. Many organizational ideas, including time awareness, goal setting, use of checklists, and breaking assignments into small steps were introduced in Chapter 4.

Additional steps to help special-needs children, steps that may also benefit all children, include providing a map of what an organized desk looks like or, at the secondary level, having students map their traffic pattern between classes. Taping a checklist of the morning routines to the student's desk helps improve task orientation. Teaching students how to take notes during a lecture, including the use of a highlighter pen for big ideas, reduces off-task behavior. It takes both parents and teachers, however, to monitor the use of such techniques before they can work.

Although you are prepared to teach many organizational techniques, be sure to provide the time to use them. For young children, take time at the end of every day to sort papers for their pocket folders with labels that say: "Goes home, stays home" and "Goes home, comes back." Upper-grade students need time at the end of every subject to complete their assignment sheet and organize homework. Give students time to begin the homework during class to allow for questions and to allow you to check their initial attempts.

If you are going to have prolonged periods of independent study, be sure there are opportunities for choice. Nothing is worse than a dull, repetitive task for causing restlessness and off-task behavior. Give students the opportunity to shift from one activity to another. On the other hand, too many choices can cause confusion and stimulate more off-task behavior. A kitchen timer provides an external prompt to promote time consciousness.

Chapter 2 provided ideas to help build a positive relationship and model positive thinking. It's helpful to remember to use specific praise, not generic, with hyperactive children because they need help to focus and to identify which behavior was praiseworthy. Develop nonverbal signals with these students to remind them to get back on task—verbal reminders may cause them embarrassment in front of peers.

Inclusive classrooms mean that you need to modify some tasks. For example, rote memorization is especially difficult for the ADD student, so try the multiplication tables or addition facts set to music. Phonemic awareness, phonics games, and nursery rhymes set to music are available on tape for young children. You may need to shorten some assignments to fit your inclusive classroom (think quality, not quantity).

Modify how students may accomplish an assignment. When I visit special education classrooms, I am fascinated by the variety of positions students take while working on an assignment. Seldom are students found in a chair. Some are standing over their desks; others are spread out on the floor. In addition to room arrangement ideas discussed in Chapter 3, individual desks are often superior to tables for the ADD/ADHD child. You might try providing headphones to block out extraneous sounds and increase task orientation. Some teachers have found having a podium in the room (for students) allows students to stand comfortably while they work.

Because ADD/ADHD children have not internalized self-talk, they require more external prompts and cues about rules, time intervals, how to break tasks down, and to anticipate future events (Barkley, 1998). Normally, a student with good metacognitive skills uses inner dialogue to check the clock to see if he'll finish on time, talks to himself about all the steps he needs to accomplish the task, and anticipates problems and works out ways to minimize them.

With an ADD/ADHD child, teachers and parents need to externalize these cues, providing verbal and visual prompts.

Anger

Look back at the list of misbehaviors. How many of them may have been the result of uncontrolled anger or rage? Who taught these children how to be angry? Is it possible that society is rein-forcing the behaviors that are problematic in the classroom? Terms like road rage or going postal were unheard of 20 years ago. What's modeled at home when the telephone solicitor calls in the middle of dinner? Because it's so easy to remain anonymous in this hectic, fast-paced life, we feel we can yell or throw a tantrum to get what we want.

Blame for the increase in anger-related problems has been directed to television, video games, and movies. A *U.S. News & World Report* (Streisand, 1999) article says that before the age of 18, children have seen 40,000 dramatized murders and 200,000 other dramatized acts of violence. There has been an increase in violent acts on prime time TV from 57 percent in 1994 to 66 percent in 1998. The problem is not getting better and is not going away.

Another *U.S. News & World Report* (Leo, 1999) article is more than blatant in its criticism of video games:

- The chief form of play for millions of youngsters is making large numbers of people die.
- A study of 900 students from 4th to 8th grade found that almost half of the children said their favorite electronic games involve violence.
- Point-and-shoot video games have the same effect as military strategies used to break down a soldier's aversion to killing.
- More realistic touches in video games help blur the boundary between fantasy and reality.
- We have our children on murder simulators.

Unlike television, video games allow the player to commit the violent act—feeling the thrill and excitement. And, unlike television where you just observe the violence, the video game participant directly experiences a reward for engaging in video violence. Violence is glamorized. Even the good guys commit violent acts. If you imagine that these repeated acts of aggression set up a script in the mind, children begin to see aggression as normal—almost an overlearned habit. They become desensitized to violence and the pain of others. Our job is to help children rewrite their scripts. Help them question what they see on television by asking:

• Does television violence contribute to real-life violence or to make kids insensitive to real human suffering?

• What did you learn from watching this program?

• How could you rewrite the script, solving the problem without resorting to violence?

Practicing Self-Control. Take time to teach anger management when students are not angry. You can't change an automatic aggressive response when students are emotionally involved. Students can list triggers or what makes them feel certain ways, but they also need a list of ways to reduce their angry feelings and to cool down. Teach them deep breathing techniques and how to use distractions and self-talk. Students need techniques for expressing anger appropriately. They need skills like mediation, compromise, negotiation, refusal, how to respond to teasing, how to disagree in an appropriate way, and how to problem solve. For elementary students, use activities to explore problem solving, anger management, feelings, tattling vs. reporting, put-ups or compliments, listening, manners, and sharing (Cummings, 1993).

There is ample evidence that training in anger management works. One study on the effects of peer mediation training with elementary students on handling school conflicts found that 74

The longer you keep your temper the more it will improve.

—*Source unknown*

percent of the conflicts were over preferences (e.g., what game to play, which activity to do first) and possession or access (who had control of books, computers, athletic equipment), 16 percent were over physical aggression, and 9 percent over insults or put-downs. (Johnson et al., 1995). Without training, these students found either win-lose solutions or got adult intervention. With training, students were able to negotiate and mediate and find new solutions to conflicts—a win-win outcome. A review of the project I have worked with is in the Appendix. (See Goleman, 1995, Appendix F, for a review of social-emotional literacy programs that have empirical results.)

Anger management strategies can be integrated across the curriculum. For example, try putting reminders for anger management to music. Music has healing qualities. If primary students know the melody to "If you're happy and you know it," change the words to

Unless both sides win, no agreement can be permanent.

—JIMMY CARTER

> If you're mad and you know it, make a choice.
>   (What choice?)
> If you're mad and you know it; you don't want to
>   blow it.
> If you're mad and you know it, make a choice.
>   (What choice?)

Each verse adds a step to consider:
> 2. If you're mad and you know it, count to 10. (9, 10)
> 3. If you're mad and you know it, walk away. (I'm gone.)
> 4. If you're mad and you know it, talk it out. (I feel . . .)

Bully Proofing. Give kids concrete steps to use when bullied. They need to know what to say and what to do. Suggest that they use the following approaches to overcome bullying.

• Identify the behavior: It's mean for you to make fun of me. You need to stop.

• Use humor. If someone calls you a name, say: You don't even know me. Wait until you get to know me before you decide what to call me.

- Agree with the remark: Yeah, I agree. You might be right!
- Just walk away.
- Use positive self-talk: I'm glad I don't feel the way she does.

Fear of bullies is more real today than in the past because weapons are often easily accessible. Because bullies want to fight, we teach children how to take the wind out of their sails by agreeing with them or using humor.

Listening. Modeling listening behavior—not an angry response—when a student is angry shows a rational way to deal with strong emotions: "You must be very angry right now. Would you tell me about it?" In our interviews with students, they often say that it's not OK to be angry. Our job is to teach that all feelings are fine, but all behaviors are not. We can respond, "I would be angry, too, if that happened to me. We know that it's not OK to hurt others or their property, so what else could we do?"

Gottman (1997) calls this "emotional coaching." He believes that we should view a child's negative emotions as an opportunity for teaching. First, are you tuned in to the student's emotion? An inner-city high school teacher read the body language of her students as both irritated and angry at the beginning of class. She asked what was going on and found that the school administration was doing a weapons and drug search that period. Instead of launching into her lesson for the day, she used the opportunity to listen empathetically to student concerns and to help them verbally label the emotions they were feeling. She shared how she felt when going through the detectors at the airport, sometimes setting them off with her jewelry and having to have a second search conducted. The class worked on the problem of how to make the search more effective and efficient.

*Become the
lesson you
would teach.*

—LEONARD ROY FRANK

Depression

Depression can stem from many things, large and small. Watch your reaction—and your students' reactions—and you may see clues to depression. You know it's a bad day when

- The slightest annoyance—bumping into you in line, taking your pencil—turns into a big deal.
- You feel like you don't have a friend in the world.
- The assignment is due but your mind keeps wandering.
- Your friends just look at you and say "What's wrong?"
- The teacher gives you "the look" to get you to work but somehow you can't even pick up the pencil.

We've all had days like those. For some of our students, however, every day is a bad day. Depression is reaching epidemic proportions, particularly among the very young. Worse yet, fewer than half of these children are receiving treatment. How many children are involved? Again, estimates vary. In their book, *Help Me, I'm Sad*, authors Fassler and Dumas (1997) believe that "one in four youngsters will experience a serious episode of depression by the time they reach their eighteenth birthday" (p. 2). The teenage suicide rate alone has tripled in the last 30 years. Fassler and Dumas point out that many of the symptoms of depression show up as misbehavior in the classroom:

- Preschoolers: overactivity; low tolerance for frustration
- School-age children: unprovoked hostility or aggression, refusal or reluctance to attend school, power struggles, sleeping in class, drop in grades, little interest in playing with others
- Adolescents: refusing to participate in school events, self-mutilation, antisocial or delinquent behavior, cheating, refusing to work in a small group, restlessness, excessive moodiness, difficulty

We are going to have to find a way to immunize people against the kind of thinking that leads to self-devastation.

—JONAS SALK

getting along with teachers or peers, extreme sensitivity to rejection or failure

In addition to seeking help for these students, there are things we can do in the classroom to help reverse the feelings of hopelessness and despair. Pessimistic thoughts and learned helplessness are often precursors to depression. Learning to think optimistically can safeguard students against depression (Seligman, 1995).

Having Friends. The Choate Depression Inventory for Children (Fassler & Dumas, 1997) can help you recognize the symptoms of depression. Many of the items revolve around having friends: "I don't have many friends. I don't like playing with other kids. Other kids don't like me. I feel lonely. Other kids have more fun than I do." The behaviors of shy and depressed children may set up a vicious sequence: 1) the child looks away, avoiding eye contact; 2) other kids interpret this as a snub and begin to avoid that child—on the playground, in the halls; 3) now, instead of attending or participating in class, the child is wondering why he has no friends; 4) lack of attending leads to academic failure and often, misbehavior.

SMILE: One tool we use to help students avoid the sequence leading to misbehavior is to teach them SMILE for making friends. (Adapted from Horn, 1997)

Friendship needs no words—it is solitude delivered from the anguish of loneliness.

—DAG HAMMARSKJOLD

S = smile

M = meet and greet: "Hi, My name is . . ."

I = invite that person to speak using Ws (who, what, where, when, why, how): "What school did you attend last year?"

L = listen and learn more about that person

E = eye contact says you care

In the lesson, we role play situations where the skill can be used and then have students keep a journal describing situations where they've tried the skill. Students are given quotes as journal prompts:

- "If you meet a person without a smile, give them one of yours" (Source unknown)
- "You miss 100 percent of the shots you never take" (Wayne Gretzky)
- "Many a friendship is lost for lack of speaking" (Source unknown)

Goleman (1995) reports that coaching unpopular children in friendship building skills removes them from the rejected category. Not having friends by the 3rd grade is a predictor of social-emotional problems in adolescence. The headline of a *USA Today* newspaper article (Peterson, 1999) "Losing popularity battle can cause lasting pain" is a sad reminder of this fact. The article notes that in most of the school shootings in the past few years the gunmen "felt like outsiders, taunted by peers." The labeling of students begins in the primary grades and often sticks with the children throughout school. This only underscores how important it is to set up a community of learners who feel bonded and connected. The need to belong is so strong that students may feel it's better to belong to a gang than to belong to no one at all.

The teacher alone can't help students connect, but empathy building activities are helpful.

Optimistic Thinking. When Dr. Seuss (1990) wrote his book, *Oh, the Places You'll Go!*, his message was one of optimism: If you try, you will succeed. I gave the book to my children when they graduated from law school, perhaps to counter the gloomy outlook of finding a job in an already overcrowded legal field. In his book, *The Optimistic Child* (1995), Seligman cites the power of an optimistic outlook on life: better personal control physical health, school success, and more resilience. Contrast that to the pessimist who feels hopeless, fails to persevere at anything, fails more frequently, achieves less at school, and has poor physical health. Think

To cease to be loved is for the child practically synonymous with ceasing to live.

—Dr. Karl Menninger

of the improvement in classroom behaviors if we could teach students that "It's all in your head!"—that our habits of thinking can lead to success or to failure.

Seligman provides tools for parents and teachers to teach optimism. My favorite is teaching the ABCs of thought catching.

A = Adversity (What is the problem? Also describe who, when, and where)

B = Belief (Why did it happen? Your interpretation of the cause of the problem.)

C = Consequences (What did you do and how did you feel after the adversity or problem?)

For example, A (adversity) might be someone cutting in front of you in traffic, causing you to slam on your brakes. B (belief) is that the person did it purposely, to bug you. C (consequence) is that you feel angry and may want to get even. Try catching that thought and reframing it. What if you believed the person who cut you off didn't see you because he was rushing a pregnant wife to the hospital? Now how would you feel and react? Covey (1997) says that responsibility means we are "response able"—able to choose our response to any adversity. Seligman has added an extra variable—we must first choose how we think about the cause of an adversity and the overt response follows accordingly. This is a great activity for students of all ages. Try it during class meetings or at a teachable moment. Seligman provides dozens of practice examples, similar to the ones found in Figure 6.1, to use with students.

The optimist sees problems as temporary while the pessimist sees them as permanent and takes them personally. A pessimistic habit of thinking is a risk factor for depression. Examples of pessimistic thought is when a student thinks that he's a loser, stupid, and will never have friends, that is a risk factor for depression. With practice, we can teach kids how to "catch their thoughts" and build the

✄ Figure 6.1
PRACTICING THE ABCs

Use these examples of Ⓐ = Adversity, Ⓑ = Belief, and Ⓒ = Consequences with your students to help them understand how to change their thinking and empower them with optimism.

Ⓐ He bumped into me in the hall.
Ⓑ He did it on purpose. He was trying to start a fight.
Ⓒ I'll show him. He'll get that fight he's looking for. (You're angry.)
   OR
Ⓑ I think he looks so preoccupied he didn't even see me.
Ⓒ I'll just ignore it this time. (You feel OK)

Ⓐ She took my pencil.
Ⓑ She thinks she can steal and get away with it.
Ⓒ A tugging war begins as you grab it back. You feel angry.
   OR
Ⓑ Maybe she mistook my pencil for hers. They do look alike.
Ⓒ You tell her it's OK if she needs to borrow your pencil.

Ⓐ Trina called me a slob.
Ⓑ I'll never do anything right. I know she doesn't like me.
Ⓒ You start crying and run away. (You feel sad.)
   OR
Ⓑ I'm glad I have plenty of friends already. I wouldn't want someone to be my friend who says cruel things.
Ⓒ You feel OK.

Ⓐ Your teacher picks Lateesha to help her.
Ⓑ I'm never picked to do anything fun. She likes Lateesha better.
Ⓒ You feel sad and depressed.
   OR
Ⓑ I was picked last month. I guess it's her turn.
Ⓒ I feel OK.

resilience they need to combat the normal stresses of adolescence.

Daniel Amen (1998) has a similar technique for warding off depression called Kill the ANTs. ANTs, automatic negative thoughts, cause your brain to release chemicals that cause your body to react—your muscles become tense, heart rate increases, and you perspire. Amen has identified nine species of ANTs that are harmful to our thinking and our health (p. 64):

1) Attributing a sense of permanence to any bad event (always or never thinking)

2) Focusing on the negative in any situation

3) Fortune-telling or anticipating the worst in any event

4) Mind reading or thinking you know what others are thinking

5) Thinking with your feelings, not using rational thought

6) Guilt-beating, for example, "I should . . . " "I ought to . . . "

7) Labeling, or using negative labels for yourself and others (creep, nerd)

8) Personalizing and assuming negative events are a personal insult directed toward you.

9) Blaming and externalizing the cause, blaming others.

To prevent the ANTs from taking over your life, Amen suggests feeding them to your anteater. That is, to recognize what kind of ANT it is (species), and kill the ANT by talking back to the irrational, illogical thought. Figure 6.2 shows how this model works.

An optimist expects his dreams to come true; a pessimist expects his nightmares to come true.

—Oscar Wilde

Interventions

You do have to pick your battles. School policy dictates which misbehaviors require an automatic suspension, expulsion, or trip to the office. Minor misbehaviors can be handled with The Law of Least Intervention—using the least amount of interruption to the learning environment. Eye contact, physical presence, "the look," or a pause in teaching can eliminate minor problems.

✎ Figure 6.2
KILLING THE ANTS

Use these examples of ANTs to help your students identify
and work around ANTs in their lives.

ANT	Species	Kill the ANT
You gave me a *D* on this assignment.	Blaming	I need to take more time on the next assignment to bring up my grade.
The kids are going to make fun of me when I do this role play.	Fortune telling	Then again, they might like it.
I'll never have any friends.	Always or never thinking	We'll make up and be friends again soon.

For chronic misbehaviors, reteaching a skill may be the solution.
The authoritative teacher balances nurturing with setting limits.
When students make poor choices, your job is to assist them in
becoming more responsible. For example, the student who turns in
late assignments could be guided through a problem process by fill-
ing out a questionnaire or during a student-teacher conference
(Figure 6.3). The first time this happens, the problem solving is
between teacher and student. If that doesn't work, students take the
process home to parents and a parent signature is required.

Action Plans. For general misbehavior in the classroom, a similar problem-solving approach is used. Have the student write out
the action plan. Prompts for reflection could be:

Example 1

- I wish I could improve . . .
- I need to improve this because . . .
- I will try . . .
- I will make restitution by . . .

Example 2

- As I write this, I am feeling . . . because . . .
- I am writing this because I chose to . . .
- A better choice would have been to . . .
- To prevent this from happening again I could . . .

Example 3

- Our class agreed to follow the "Three Rs: Rights, Respect, and Responsibility."
  - I need to make better choices about . . . because . . .
  - This won't happen again because I will . . .

Example 4

- I will try to explain my problem with the Ws (who, what, when, where, how, and why).
  - I can fix this problem by . . .
  - This is what happened . . .
  - This is what should have happened . . .
  - This is my plan for the future . . .

Example 5

- I feel confident that I can make it work because . . .
- We were fighting because . . .
- The fight actually began when . . .
- It wouldn't have continued if . . .

Do not use a hatchet to remove a fly from your friend's forehead.

—CHINESE PROVERB

✂ **Figure 6.3**
LATE ASSIGNMENT FORM

Use this form to help students identify why their assignments are late (and to accept the blame and explain the reason, as necessary). The form also help both you and the student track late assignments.

Directions: Please fill out this form completely and staple it to your late assignment for credit.

Name _____ Today's Date _____

Assignment Title or Description _____
_____

I was not able to get this assignment in on time for the reason below
(check all that apply):

❏ I was absent on _____ (dates).
❏ I left it at home.
❏ I didn't know it was due.
❏ I didn't understand the assignment.
❏ Even though I used my time in class wisely, I didn't complete it on time.
❏ I wasted my time in class and didn't complete it on time.
❏ I forgot to do it for homework.
❏ Other reasons (explain here): _____

If this assignment is not late because you were absent, list at least one thing that you can work on in the future that will help you get your assignments in on time:

1.

2.

3.

*Note: Late assignments are worth partial credit unless you have an excused absence and turn in your make-up assignment within the allotted time.

Adapted from Anne Stewart, Edmonds (WA) School District

- If we were to rewrite the scenario with a win-win ending for both of us, it would have played out like this . . .
  - We both agree to make better choices next time. (signatures)

Example 6
- I made a poor choice when I . . . I probably did it because . . . (I wanted attention, wanted to challenge the teacher, to be noticed, to get even, to avoid doing work I thought was too difficult)
  - I could achieve my goal another way by . . .
  - So, next time I will . . .
  - If I need help, I can go to . . .

When these plans don't have the desired effect of improving self-control, it's time to either involve the parents or the teacher. With very young children, the teacher is involved from the start, helping to outline a plan for improvement. With older students, the teacher is involved when the student's first attempt doesn't work and he needs alternative solutions.

My philosophy has been "Winning them over, not winning over them." The child who just loves his teacher is more likely to perform than one who feels disconnected from the classroom. When you take time to ask *why* did this happen, you'll have a class working with you, not against you. Stephen Covey's habit of "Seek first to understand, then to be understood" (1997) is the guiding principle in dealing with misbehavior. As you help your students work through the different kinds of threats (intellectual, emotional, and physical), you can help them to identify and overcome the challenges faced in the everyday classroom. The bottom line is that if you want good behavior, teach the skills for good behavior.

References

Amen, D. (1998). *Change your brain, change your life.* New York: Times Books.

Association for Supervision and Curriculum Development. (1997, May). Social and emotional learning [theme issue]. *Educational Leadership,* (54), 8.

Barkley, R. (1998, September). Attention-Deficit Hyperactivity Disorder. *Scientific American,* pp. 66–71.

Bennett, W. (Ed.). (1996). *The book of virtues.* New York: Simon & Schuster.

Bennett, W. (Ed.). (1997). *The children's book of heroes.* New York: Simon & Schuster.

Bettencourt, E., Gillett, M., Gall, M., & Hull, R. (1983). Effects of teacher enthusiasm training on student on-task behavior and achievement. *American Educational Research Journal, 30*(3), pp. 435–450.

Biro, B. (1995). *Beyond success: The 15 secrets of a winning life.* Hamilton, Montana: Pygmalion Press.

Blythe, M., & Bradbury, P. (1993). Classroom by committee. *Educational Leadership, 50*(7), 56–58.

Boettinger, H. (1969). *Moving mountains: The art of letting others see things your way.* New York: Collier Books.

Burke, J. (1993). Tackling society's problems in English class. *Educational Leadership, 50*(7), 16–18.

Canfield, J., Hansen, M., & Kirberger, K. (1997). *Chicken soup for the teenage soul.* Deerfield Beach, FL: Health Communications, Inc.

Cohen, A. (1999, May 3) A curse of cliques. *Time,* pp. 44–45.

Cohen, E. (1994). Restructuring the classroom: Conditions for productive small groups. *Review of Educational Research, 64*(1), 1–35.

Collins, M., & Tamarkin, C. (1990). *Marva Collins' way.* New York: J. P. Tarcher/Putnam.

Cooper, R., & Sawaf, A. (1996). *Executive EQ: Emotional intelligence in leadership and organizations.* New York: Grosset/Putnam.

Cooper, H. (1994). *The battle over homework: An administrator's guide to setting sound and effective policies.* Thousand Oaks, CA: Corwin Press, Inc.

Covey, S. R. (1997). *The seven habits of highly effective families.* New York: Golden Books.

Cummings, C. (1992). *Won't you ever listen?* Edmonds, WA: Teaching, Inc.

Cummings, C. (1993). *The get-alongs.* Edmonds, WA: Teaching, Inc.

Cummings, C. (1996). *Managing to teach.* Edmonds, WA: Teaching, Inc.

Cummings, C. (1990). *Managing a cooperative classroom.* Edmonds, WA: Teaching, Inc.

Curwin, R., & Mendler, A. (1999). *Discipline with dignity* (2nd ed.). Alexandria, VA: ASCD.

DeGaetano, G., & Bander, K. (1996). *Screen smarts: A family guide to media literacy.* Boston: Houghton Mifflin Co.

Deiro, J. A. (1996). *Teaching with heart: Making healthy connections with students.* Thousand Oaks, CA: Corwin Press, Inc.

Edelston, M. (1993, December). *Bottom line.* Boulder, CO: Boardroom Reports, Inc.

Fassler, D., & Dumas, L. (1997). *Help me, I'm sad.* New York: Viking.

Fuchs, D., Fuchs, L., Mathes, P., & Simmons, D. (1997). Peer-assisted learning strategies: Making classrooms more responsive to diversity. *American Educational Research Journal. 34*(1), 174–206.

Galassi, J., Gulledge, S., & Cox, N. (1997). Middle school advisories: Retrospect and prospect. *Review of Educational Research, 67*(3), 301–338.

Gathercoal, F. (1990). *Judicious discipline.* Ann Arbor, MI: Caddo Gap Press.

Glenn, H. S. & Nelsen, J. (1989). *Raising self-reliant children in a self-indulgent world.* Rocklin, CA: Prima Publishing & Communications.

Goleman, D. (1995). *Emotional intelligence: Why it can matter more than IQ.* New York: Bantam Books.

Goleman, D. (1998). *Working with emotional intelligence.* New York: Bantam Books.

Gottman, J. (1997). *The heart of parenting.* New York: Simon & Schuster.

Gutierrez, R., & Slavin, R. (1992). Achievement effects of the nongraded elementary school: A best evidence synthesis. *Review of Educational Research, 62,* 333–376.

Healy, J. (1990). *Endangered minds: Why children don't think and what we can do about it.* New York: Simon & Schuster.

Healy, J. (1994). *Your child's growing mind: A guide to brain development and learning from birth to adolescence.* New York: Doubleday.

Healy, J. (1998). *Failure to connect: How computers affect our children's minds—for better and worse.* New York: Simon & Schuster.

Hoover-Dempsey, K., & Sandler, H. (1997). Why do parents become involved in their children's education? *Review of Educational Research 67*(1), 3–42.

Horn, S. (1997). *Concrete confidence.* New York: St. Martin's Press.

Johnson, D., Johnson, R., Dudley, B., Ward, M., & Magnuson, D. (1995). The impact of peer mediation training on the management of school and home conflicts. *American Educational Research Journal. 32*(4), 829–844.

Leo, J. (1999, May 3). When life imitates video. *U.S. News & World Report.*

Lickona, T. (1991). *Educating for character: How our schools can teach respect and responsibility.* New York: Bantam Books.

Mason, D., & Burns, R. (1996). "Simply no worse and simply no better" may simply be wrong: A critique of Veenman's conclusion about multigrade classes. *Review of Educational Research. 66*(3), 307–322.

Mizer, J. E. (1964, November). *Cipher in the snow.* National Education Association Journal, pp. 8–10.

National Center for Educational Statistics (1999, January). Teacher quality: A report on the preparation and quality of public school teachers, U.S. Department of Education.

National Commission on Education. (1983). *A nation at risk: The imperative for educational reform.* Washington, D.C.: U.S. Government Printing Office.

New Standards. (1997). *Performance standards: English language arts, mathematics, science, applied learning.* Washington D.C.: National Center on Education and the Economy.

Payne, R. (1998). *A framework for understanding poverty.* Baytown, TX: RFT Publishing.

Peale, N. (1967). *Enthusiasm makes the difference.* Greenwich, CT: Fawcett Publications, Inc.

Peterson, K. (1999, April 28). Losing popularity battle can cause lasting pain. *USA Today.*

Phillips, M. (1997). What makes schools effective? A comparison of the relationships of communitarian climate and academic climate to mathematics achievement and attendance during middle school. *American Educational Research Journal, 34*(4), 633–662.

Pipho, C. (1998). The value-added side of standards. *Kappan, 79*(5), 341–2.

Ratnesar, R. (1998, September 14). Lost in the Middle, *Time.*

Resnick, M. D., Bearman, P., Blum, R., Bauman, K., Harris, K., Jones, J., Tabor, J., Beuhring, T., Sieving, R., Shew, M., Ireland, M., Bearinger, L., & Udry, J. (1997). Protecting adolescents from harm—Findings from the national longitudinal study on adolescent health. *Journal of the American Medical Association, 278*(10), 823–832.

Schunk, D. H. (1991). Self-efficacy and academic motivation. *Educational Psychologist* 26, 3 & 4: 207–231.

Secretary's Commission on Achieving Necessary Skills. (1991). *What work requires of schools: A SCANS report for America 2000.* U.S. Department of Labor.

Seligman, M. E. (1995). *The optimistic child.* New York: Houghton Mifflin Co.

Seuss, Dr. (1990). *Oh, the places you'll go!* New York: Random House.

Shapiro, L. E. (1997). *How to raise a child with a high EQ.* New York: Harper Collins.

Silverstein, S. (1996). *Falling up.* New York: Harper Collins.

Silverstein, S. (1981). *A light in the attic.* New York: Harper Collins.

Spady, W., & Marshall, K. (1991). Beyond traditional outcome-based education. *Educational Leadership 49*(2), 67–72.

Stanford, J. (1999). *Victory in our schools.* New York: Bantam Books.

Steinberg, L. (1996). *Beyond the classroom: Why school reform has failed and what parents need to do.* New York: Simon & Schuster.

Stevens, R., & Slavin, R. (1995). The cooperative elementary school: Effects on students' achievement, attitudes, and social relations. *American Educational Research Journal. 32*(2), 321–351.

Streisand, B. (1999, June 14). Lawyers, guns, money. *U.S. News & World Report.*

Sylwester, R. (2000). *A biological brain in a cultural classroom.* Thousand Oaks, CA: Corwin Press, Inc.

Veenman, S. (1995). Cognitive and noncognitive effects of multigrade and multi-age classes: A best-evidence synthesis. *Review of Educational Research, 65*(4), 319–381.

Yocum, T., & Tibbets, B. (1999). [ASCD Inquiry Kit]. Curriculum integration. Alexandria, VA: Association for Supervision and Curriculum Development.

Wang, M., Haertel, G., & Walberg, H. (1994). What helps students learn? *Educational Leadership 51*(4), 74–79.

Washington State Commission on Student Learning. (1998). *Essential academic learning requirements.* Olympia, WA: Author.

Wilson, S. B. (1994). *Goal setting.* New York: AMACOM, a division of American Management Association.

Appendix
Research on Efficacy of Teaching Practices

Critical questions about the efficacy of the teaching practices and strategies presented in this book have been explored in two long-term prevention trials funded by the National Institute on Drug Abuse. This appendix provides summaries of studies conducted by University of Washington's Social Development Research Group that support such teaching practices along with other intervention components to build strong positive bonds with students. The studies summarized here report on the short-term and long-term efficacy of comprehensive prevention interventions targeting the school, family, and individual. The interventions are guided by the Society Development Model (Catalano & Hawkins, 1996), a theory that explains the development of both prosocial and antisocial behavior.

The Seattle Social Development Project

The Seattle Social Development Program (SSDP) is a three-part intervention for teachers, parents, and students in grades 1 to 6. It is a universal prevention program. The SSDP has been evaluated in Seattle elementary and middle schools by independent and objective standards in program and comparison schools. Seven evaluative studies of the Seattle social development interventions have been conducted. These studies found direct effects of the intervention on childhood and adolescent problem behaviors, such as aggression, violence, drug use, delinquency, and school misbehavior, in addition to direct effects of the intervention on risk and protective factors. An independent cost-benefit analysis estimated that projected reductions in violent crimes resulting from SSDP would result in reduced taxpayer costs and payments to crime victims. The analysis suggests that for every participant, the savings is $3,268. The following information contains the results from the seven studies.

Results

• As a result of participating in the combined social development intervention in grades 1 and 2, boys were less aggressive and demonstrated less externalizing antisocial behavior; girls were less self-destructive when compared with their counterparts in a control group.

• As a result of participating in the combined social development intervention in grades 1–4, children were less likely to initiate alcohol use and less likely to initiate delinquency. These children also reported better family management, family communication, family involvement, attachment to family, school reward, school attachment, and school commitment, as compared with controls.

• As a result of participating in the full social development intervention in grades 1–6, low-income girls were less likely to initiate cigarette use and more likely to report classroom and team learning opportunities, they reported more classroom participation, more bonding and commitment to school, and fewer opportunities to get marijuana. Low-income boys were more likely to report improved social skills, school work and commitment to school, to have better achievement test scores and grades, and less likely to have antisocial peers, as compared with low-income controls.

• As a result of assignment to intervention classrooms in grades

5 and 6 (with effects of intervention at grades 1–4 controlled), student has higher achievement test scores at the end of grade 6 when compared with those in control classrooms. Also, more teacher implementation of targeted teaching practices led to more classroom involvement, more perceived classroom reinforcement, and more bonding to school, as compared with students and teachers in the control group.

• As a result of participating in the full social development intervention in grades 1–6, the decline in school bonding through adolescence was slower, with higher school bonding evident at ages 16 and 18, as compared with controls.

• As a result of participating in the full social development intervention in grades 1–6, based on reduction in self-reported violent offenses at age 18, a reduction in felony arrests by age 25 was projected, as compared with the control group. The full intervention was cost-effective, producing a positive return per student to both taxpayers and crime victims.

Raising Healthy Children

The Raising Healthy Children Project (RHC) extends earlier work from the Seattle Social Development Project (Hawkins et al., 1992; O'Donnell et al., 1995). Ten urban elementary schools were randomly assigned to program or comparison condition resulting in 562 program students and 478 control students. Raising Healthy Children offers a comprehensive program with strategies that focus on these three domains.

• The school intervention strategy provides a series of instructional improvement workshops and classroom coaching for teachers. The workshops are designed to increase students' commitment and attachment to school while reducing academic failure.

• The family intervention strategy offers parenting workshops and home-based services to enhance parents' skills in child rearing, in order to increase attachment and commitment to the family and decrease family management problems.

• The peer intervention strategy offers opportunities for children to learn and practice social and emotional skills in the classroom and in social situations.

Results

• Teachers were independently observed using more instructional practices targeted by the intervention that promote student involvement, and social skills reinforcement, when compared with control teachers. These included proactive classroom management, motivation strategies, student involvement, cooperative learning, reading, and social skills reinforcement.

• Summary scores of the classroom observations support that the target instructional practices are related to student behaviors in the hypothesized manner.

• Teachers' report of student (908 students) behavior demonstrated both academic and behavioral improvements for students in the experimental condition, suggesting that the intervention is having a desirable effect on early risk and protective factors, have reduced risk for later chronic problem behaviors and had greater protection.

• Parents' report of intervention students show higher levels of social competency for those students than control students.

Compiled by Kevin Haggerty, Social Development Research Group, University of Washington

Sources

Abbott, R. D., O'Donnell, J., Hawkins, J. D., Hill, K. G., Kosterman, R., Catalano, R.F. (1998). Changing teaching practices to promote achievement and bonding to school. *American Journal of Orthopsychiatry 68*(4), pp. 542–552.

Catalano, R. F., Harachi, T. W., Abbott, R. D., & Haggerty, K. P. (Unpublished manuscript). Raising healthy children through enhancing social development in elementary school: Results after 1.5 years.

Harachi, T. W., Abbott, R. D., Catalano, R. F., & Haggerty, K. P. (1999). Validating an observational system to examine program implementation. *Journal of Community Psychology, 27*(5), 711–731.

Harachi, T. W., Catalano, R. F., Fleming, C., Abbott, R. D., Haggerty, K. P. (1998, June). Results from a school-based program supporting positive youth development. Paper presented at the Society for Prevention Research, Park City, UT.

Hawkins, J. D., Catalano, R. F., Jones, G., & Fine, D. N. (1987). Delinquency prevention through parent training: Results and issues from work in progress. In J. Q., Wilson & G. C. Loury (eds.), *From children to citizens: Families, schools, and delinquency prevention* (Vol. 3, pp. 186–204). New York: Springer-Verlag.

Hawkins, J. D., Catalano, R. F., Kosterman, R., Abbott, R., & Hill, K. G. (1999). Preventing adolescent health-risk behaviors by strengthening protection during childhood. *Archives of Pediatric and Adolescent Medicine, 153*(3), 226–234.

Hawkins, J. D., Catalano, R. F., Morrison, D. M., O'Donnell, J., Abbott, R., & Day, L. E. (1992). The Seattle Social Development Project: Effects of the first four years on protective factors and problem behaviors. In Joan McCord & R. Tremblay (Eds.). *Preventing anti-social behavior: Interventions from birth through adolescence.* New York: Guilford Press.

Hawkins, J., Doueck, H., & Lishner, D. (1988). Changing teaching practices in mainstream classrooms to improve bonding and behavior of low achievers. *American Educational Research Journal, 25*(1), 31–50.

Hawkins, J. D., Guo, J., Hill, K., Battin-Pearson, S. (in press). Long-term effects of the Seattle social development intervention on the growth in school bonding. *Examining the Gateway Hypothesis Stages: Pathways of Drug Involvement.* Cambridge University Press.

Hawkins, J., Von Cleve, E., Catalano, R. (1991). Reducing early childhood aggression: Results of a primary prevention program. *Journal of the American Academy of Child and Adolescent Psychiatry, 30*(2), 208–217.

O'Donnell, J., Hawkins, J. D., Catalano, R. F., Abbott, R., & Day, L. E. (1995). Preventing school failure, drug use, and delinquency among low-income children: Long-term intervention in elementary schools. *American Journal of Orthopsychiatry, 65*(1): 87–100.

Washington State Institute for Public Policy. (1998). *Watching the bottom line: Cost effective interventions for reducing crime in Washington.* The Evergreen State College, Olympia, WA.

☙ Index

About the Author

Carol Cummings conducts workshops for parents and teachers throughout the world on motivation, social skills, effective teaching, reading and writing strategies, classroom management, and managing diverse classrooms. She has taught in the classroom, conducted research on at-risk learners, and written more 15 books for teachers and children. Her first two books, *Teaching Makes a Difference* and *Managing to Teach*, have sold more than 250,000 copies. Her children's series, *The Get Alongs,* is used to teach social-emotional skills to young children throughout the United States. Cummings teaches for both the University of Washington and Seattle Pacific University. Her doctorate is in Curriculum and Instruction from the University of Washington.

She can be reached at P.O. Box 788, Edmonds, WA 98020. E-mail: cummings@wolfenet.com.

Related ASCD Resources: Classroom Management

ASCD stock numbers are noted in parentheses.

Audiotapes
Applying Brain/Stress Research to Classroom Management by Robert Sylwester (#297188)
Brain Research Applied to Classroom Management by Gene Van Tassell (#200126)
Changing the Ways Teachers and Students Think About and Respond to Classroom Management by H. Jerome Freiberg, Armandina Farias, Silvia McClure, and Wanda Watson (#296180)
Development of a Peer Coaching Classroom Management Program by Terry Elfrink (#298106)
Effective Discipline: Getting Beyond Rewards and Punishments by Marvin Marshall (#297190)
Insights on Better Classroom Management from Brain Research (#299194)
Student Discipline in Democratic Classrooms by Antwanette Hill and H. Jerome Freiberg (#297054)

Print Products
As Tough as Necessary: Countering Violence, Aggression, and Hostility in Our Schools by Richard L. Curwin and Allen N. Mendler (#197017)
Beyond Discipline: From Compliance to Community by Alfie Kohn (#196075)
Classroom Management by Robert Hanson (ASCD Professional Inquiry Kit #998059)
Classroom Management/Positive School Climate (ASCD Topic Pack #198219)
Differentiating Instruction for Mixed-Ability Classrooms by Carol Ann Tomlinson (ASCD Professional Inquiry Kit #196213)
Discipline with Dignity 2nd ed. by Richard L. Curwin and Allen N. Mendler (#199235)
Managing to Teach: A Guide to Classroom Management, 2nd ed. by Carol Cummings (#300268)
Talk it Out: Conflict Resolution in the Elementary Classroom by Barbara Porro (#196018)

Videotapes
Catch Them Being Good: Reinforcement in the Classroom, featuring Pat Wolfe (3-tape series #614162)
Differentiating Instruction (2-tape series #497023)
Early Childhood Education: Classroom Management and Curriculum Organization (#614221)
Managing Today's Classroom (3-tape series #498027)

For additional resources, visit us on the World Wide Web (http://www.ascd.org), send an e-mail message to member@ascd.org, call the ASCD Service Center (1-800-933-ASCD or 703-578-9600, then press 2), send a fax to 703-575-5400, or write to Information Services, ASCD, 1703 N. Beauregard St., Alexandria, VA 22311-1714 USA.